Community-Engaged Performance Tours

Community-Engaged Performance Tours addresses the role of performance touring as a form of classroom and community engagement. Performance tours have long been a part of the collegiate and high school music ensemble experience, bringing student bands, choirs, and orchestras into connection with a wide variety of audiences, venues, and cultural contexts. This book presents a new approach to the performance tour that integrates touring with community engagement and service-learning. Emphasizing reciprocity, cross-cultural exchange, and global awareness, the author addresses how visiting ensembles can work *with* host communities instead of performing *for* them. The book includes student and community perspectives and case studies from the author's experience leading university wind symphony tours in Haiti and the Dominican Republic, and provides a practical and hands-on model for ensemble leaders and educators.

James Spinazzola is Barbara & Richard T. Silver Associate Professor of Music and Director of Winds at Cornell University.

Community-Engaged Performance Tours
A Guide for Music Ensemble Directors and Educators

James Spinazzola

NEW YORK AND LONDON

First published 2024
by Routledge
605 Third Avenue, New York, NY 10158

and by Routledge
4 Park Square, Milton Park, Abingdon, Oxon, OX14 4RN

Routledge is an imprint of the Taylor & Francis Group, an informa business

© 2024 James Spinazzola

The right of James Spinazzola to be identified as author of this work has been asserted in accordance with sections 77 and 78 of the Copyright, Designs and Patents Act 1988.

All rights reserved. No part of this book may be reprinted or reproduced or utilised in any form or by any electronic, mechanical, or other means, now known or hereafter invented, including photocopying and recording, or in any information storage or retrieval system, without permission in writing from the publishers.

Trademark notice: Product or corporate names may be trademarks or registered trademarks, and are used only for identification and explanation without intent to infringe.

Library of Congress Cataloging-in-Publication Data
Names: Spinazzola, James, author.
Title: Community-engaged performance tours : a guide for music ensemble directors and educators / James Spinazzola.
Description: New York : Routledge, 2023. | Includes bibliographical references and index.
Identifiers: LCCN 2023012668 (print) | LCCN 2023012669 (ebook) | ISBN 9781032244648 (hardback) | ISBN 9781032244655 (paperback) | ISBN 9781003278696 (ebook)
Subjects: LCSH: Concert tours—Social aspects. | Community development—Study and teaching. | Service learning.
Classification: LCC ML3916 .S75 2023 (print) | LCC ML3916 (ebook) | DDC 306.4/842—dc23/eng/20230526
LC record available at https://lccn.loc.gov/2023012668
LC ebook record available at https://lccn.loc.gov/2023012669

ISBN: 978-1-032-24464-8 (hbk)
ISBN: 978-1-032-24465-5 (pbk)
ISBN: 978-1-003-27869-6 (ebk)

DOI: 10.4324/9781003278696

Typeset in Times New Roman
by Apex CoVantage, LLC

Contents

	Introduction	1
1	A Concise History of Community Engagement in Higher Education	8
2	Traditional and Community-Engaged Performance Tours: From Tourism to Partnership	21
3	Foundations of a Community-Engaged Performance Tour: Planning and Partnership	35
4	The Pedagogy of Community-Engaged Performance Tours	46
5	Case Study: The Cornell Wind Symphony in Haiti and the Dominican Republic	67
6	The Logistics of Leading a Community-Engaged Performance Tour	90
	Epilogue	104
	Index	*113*

Introduction

My Story

Our bus sat for hours without moving. Tropical heat and a steady rain left us feeling as though we were in a sauna. Given that it was the Cornell University Wind Symphony's first tour of Haiti, the 50 student musicians were rolling with the punches rather well. I was trying to do the same, but as their conductor, I felt responsible for having led them into what was quickly becoming a mess. The date was January 2017. My students and I were in the town of Milot, near the northern coastal city of Cap-Haïtien, en route to a gala concert at Sans-Souci Palace.[1] Everything was on track—until we got caught by the maddening traffic.

Even under ideal circumstances, getting from one place to another in Haiti can be absurdly difficult. Cities have no municipal public transportation systems, and functioning traffic signals are a cause for celebration. Something as simple as traveling to a performance can become an adventure. "Haitian time," a seemingly casual approach to temporal organization, complicates matters. Regardless of published schedules, few events in Haiti start on time. As our evening wore on, my students and I came to appreciate a common Haitian adage: *pa gen anyen ap travay, men tout bagay ap travay* (nothing works, but everything works out).

Despite the light but steady rain falling on audience members, our partners from the Holy Trinity Music School (HTMS) in Port-au-Prince kept the concert going in our absence. The school's Philharmonic Orchestra played the same pieces multiple times, and the concert organizers had enlisted the talents of local performers—apparently including a fire-swallowing act I'm sorry to have missed!

Meanwhile, our journey of a few miles included countless delays and a brief detour that involved students riding through the rain in the beds of pickup trucks provided at a moment's notice by the owner of our hotel. When we finally arrived, we were more than 2 hours late for our own concert. The program my colleagues and I had carefully prepared and rehearsed was impossible to realize.

My students were exhausted but thrilled by the prospect of finally performing and ran to the stage. The performance went beautifully. We presented one piece in collaboration with the HTMS Philharmonic Orchestra and choirs: *Mesi Bondye* (Thank God). Following the audience's applause, the piece evolved organically into a jam session featuring *rara*[2] percussion rhythms and riffs shared among the wind players. The atmosphere was electric. The music and dancing continued until the hired production company turned off the lights.

Afterward, I was finally able to share a few quiet moments with HTMS director and orchestra conductor The Rev. David César, longtime HTMS supporter and concert coproducer The Rev. Stephen Davenport (ret.), former Haitian Minister of Tourism and concert coproducer Patrick Delatour, Yale University Director of Bands, Thomas Duffy,[3] and many other individuals, without whom the remarkable concert would not have been possible. The day had been taxing and exhilarating and was emblematic of the entire tour. Our challenges were significant—from the effort, funding, logistics, and security measures required to transport 50 student musicians into an at-risk foreign country, to establishing personal and institutional relationships, to overcoming language and culture barriers. However, the rewards—for our students and us—inspired us to agree to do it again.

Photo 0.1 Cornell University Wind Symphony and Holy Trinity Music School Philharmonic Orchestra

Joint performance, Sans-Souci Palace, January 2017

Port-au-Prince is chaotic at the best of times, but an even more disordered atmosphere greeted the Cornell Wind Symphony (CWS) on its second tour in 2019. Recent political scandals had further stressed a fragile infrastructure, creating increased governmental instability and civil unrest. When I told friends that we were returning to the island, they sometimes asked, "why *Haiti*"? I somewhat expected that question because, then and now, virtually every article about Haiti in the global press reminds readers that it is the poorest nation in the western hemisphere.[4] Haiti has been victimized by natural disasters, global oppression, political corruption, and mismanagement. The U.S. State Department frequently advises against traveling to Haiti due to widespread crime, civil unrest, and political instability.[5] Although Haiti is home to 11 million people and only about 800 miles south of Florida, most U.S. news outlets cover the country only under the most tragic circumstances. The Editorial Board of the *New York Times* wrote, "Life has never been easy in Haiti, and that may be why the current nightmare there is not getting more attention" (November 2019).

Nevertheless, the CWS continued to build relationships with Haitian institutions. The University of the Aristide Foundation[6] invited us to perform on campus in January 2019 as part of a ceremony to honor the estimated 200,000 people who perished in the tragic 2010 earthquake that devastated the country. A member of the ensemble reflected on the experience:

> I was confused at this afternoon's concert when we began playing . . . while a lady was speaking in French at the podium. Were we interrupting her? But then my heart broke when she started listing the names of university students' friends and family members who passed away in the 2010 earthquake. I noticed the procession of students holding white carnations. They walked down the center aisle of the auditorium and placed them in a glass vase at the front. A tribute to lives lost. It is so easy to be detached when people are hit by a natural disaster that does not directly affect us. It is so hard to fathom the weight of the aftermath. But experiences like today bring context to tragedy and invite us to contemplate and respect others' pain.
> (Vineeta Mutharaj, 2019)

Before our tour, this student, a senior majoring in Materials Science and Engineering, had known little about Haitian history and culture. Although our pre-tour activities provided essential background information, the experience of visiting Haiti on two separate tours, interacting with people, and sharing artistic creations ultimately changed her perception. Her experience helped her develop a new worldview borne by a culturally sensitive understanding and recognition of music's potential to highlight commonalities between seemingly disparate groups of people. As Vineeta wrote,

> The world needs to shift its perspective on Haiti from a sympathetic one to an empathetic one. For us, as an ensemble, music is the best way to do this. Although most of us face language barriers, all of us understand music.

Her message was profound. Empathy—the capacity to place oneself in another's position—does not develop in a vacuum but grows organically from knowledge, awareness, and understanding. Such capacity is precisely what community-engaged performance tours are designed to engender. Through these tours and related learning and reflection activities, my students and I built a frame of reference through which unfamiliar cultural environments—with Haiti as one example—can be examined with careful inquiry, fairness, and compassion. These developments were possible only through a "deep dive," precisely what community-engaged performance tours are designed to provide.

As of this writing, a confluence of events is creating global challenges greater than any since World War II. Most prominently, the COVID-19 (coronavirus) pandemic has spread to every continent and continues to leave devastating health, social, economic, and political crises. Haiti was fundamentally unprepared to confront these crises, and they quickly outpaced efforts to contain them. In July 2021, President Jovenal Moise's assassination dealt the country's fragile government another blow. The resulting power vacuum fostered an already flourishing criminal gang influence. Kidnappings became increasingly common, and many citizens abandoned parts of Port-au-Prince and fled the country. Haiti's tourism industry, which was already on life-support, nearly halted. Today, the country is virtually isolated, even from the country with which it shares the island of Hispaniola, the Dominican Republic. Haiti is in dire straits.

Amid these hardships, The Holy Trinity Music School experienced a profound loss when its director, The Rev. David César, died on June 10, 2021. David was a priest in the Episcopal Church, conductor of the school's orchestra, director of the annual HTMS summer camp, and a violist in the HTMS chamber ensemble. David was committed to using music to spread love and joy to his congregation and many students. He sacrificed much to realize that goal, and his efforts were recognized both nationally and internationally through an Honorary Doctorate in Divinity from the Berkeley Divinity School of Yale University (2013); the award-winning documentary *Serenade for Haiti* (2016), which, in part, chronicles David's work at HTMS; and numerous other accolades.

I had the privilege of knowing David for six years, and over the course of that time, he became a trusted colleague and friend. Whether we were waiting to pass through a seemingly endless Haitian roadblock, relaxing over glasses of Barbancourt rum at the Oloffson Hotel in Port-au-Prince, or planning our joint concerts, I was continually inspired by David's warmth, sincerity, humor, and dedication. Our relationship left an indelible mark on my approach to music-making, touring, and, more broadly, living in the world. I am eternally grateful to David for joining me in two remarkable musical adventures in Haiti and committing to a long-term campus–community partnership.

Introduction 5

Photo 0.2 James Spinazzola and The Rev. David César
Cap-Haïtien, Haiti, January 2017

Community-Engaged Performance Tours

Performance tours have long been integral to the collegiate and high school ensemble experience. Bands, choirs, and orchestras routinely traverse the globe, building camaraderie, exposing students to different cultures and significant venues, and sharing music and goodwill.

The musical benefits of any performance tour are well-known to both ensemble directors and tour companies. The tour represents a clear musical goal of performing for off-campus audiences, which, as a capstone project, inspires students to perform at the highest possible level. Students develop professionalism by learning to produce high-quality music regardless of the many unpredictable variables associated with touring. Depending on the tour location, students may become more informed musical interpreters by performing in historically significant venues or becoming more aware of composers' backgrounds and cultures.

Touring also offers social benefits as students have the opportunity to connect with each other on a deeper and more personal level. By traveling, dining, and making music together, they share experiences that will form the basis of enduring social memories. This fellowship, combined with music-making, fosters students' sense of unity and pride in the ensemble.

The home institution and department or school of music may also reap the benefits of ensemble tours by leveraging them toward brand recognition and recruitment initiatives. Facing outward, the students become campus ambassadors; facing inward, the ensemble's tours enhance the institution's overall educational experience.

As beneficial as traditional tours may be, students' cultural exposure is typically limited to tourism, and community relationships generally relate to one-off events rather than sustained contact or collaboration. The itinerary typically follows a "beaten path" to showcase globally recognized cultural offerings and points of interest. Few tour companies travel to challenging contexts in the Global South—countries in Asia, Africa, Latin America, and the Caribbean considered to have large populations of low or, at best, middle income compared to the Global North. The conductor and ensemble may interact with musical organizations in tour locations. However, these interactions are usually related to a single musical event, like a university orchestra working with a local choir to perform a particular musical work.

Community-engaged performance tours explore the full potential of touring by shifting the primary mission from tourism to community engagement, building sustained community partnerships rather than staging one or two concerts, and integrating musical learning goals and service-learning. These tours focus on five key factors: cross-cultural exchange, global awareness, genuine partnership with off-campus communities, reciprocity, and structured student reflection. They leverage ensemble and institutional resources toward authentic collaboration with the community to solve problems and find solutions. The educational institution and community partners are on equal footing—they share, learn, and benefit from the relationship. Music is a springboard to creating sustained partnerships *with* a community instead of a single experience *for* the community.

Community-engaged performance tours can help participants overcome cultural and language barriers, develop an informed, empathetic worldview, and foster inclusive and respectful cultures in their respective ensembles. All of this is possible without sacrificing musical goals or curricular learning outcomes.

This Book

This book is a guide for college and high school ensemble directors seeking to plan and lead community-engaged performance tours. The content includes historical context, philosophical underpinnings, essential principles, and practical suggestions. A review of current literature in the field provides background to the work's hands-on experience gained through CWS tours, student feedback, and personal reflections.

Chapter 1 presents a brief history of community engagement, engaged scholarship, and service-learning in U.S. higher education. Traditional and community-engaged performance tours are defined, compared, and contrasted in Chapter 2, which also examines tourism's effects on visitors and hosts. Chapter 3 comprises the fundamental elements of crafting a community-engaged performance tour and developing community partnerships. Chapter 4 outlines and makes a case for a pedagogy of community-engaged performance tours. I present anecdotal information, lessons learned, and student reflections from the 2017 and 2019 CWS tours of Haiti and the Dominican Republic in Chapter 5. Chapter 6 addresses myriad logistical, financial, health, and safety concerns associated with escorting a group of students to an at-risk international location. In the Epilogue, I discuss the struggles of maintaining international partnerships and share comments from community partners and students.

At the risk of sounding Pollyannish, this book is about using music to connect groups of people. Only then can we begin to understand each other.

Notes

1 Henry Cristoph, a leader in the Haitian revolution and self-proclaimed ruler of the Kingdom of Haiti, constructed Sans-Souci palace in 1813. An earthquake in 1842 left it largely in ruin, never to be rebuilt. In 1982, UNESCO designated the palace a World Heritage Site.
2 The term *rara* alternatively describes a genre of music primarily associated with Haitian Carnival, parade bands that play such music, and associated dance.
3 Duffy and six members of the Yale Concert Band participated in the Cornell Wind Symphony tour.
4 This is a broad misrepresentation of Haiti's position. More accurately, Haiti is the nation "most impoverished by the effects of white supremacy" (Degraff, 2022).
5 The State Department lists four travel advisory levels: 1) exercise normal precautions, 2) exercise increased caution, 3) reconsider travel, and 4) do not travel. The Wind Symphony traveled to Haiti during a Level Two advisory in 2017 and Level Three in 2019. Our decision to travel was based on advice from my Haitian colleagues and information I gathered on while visiting the country and was vetted by Cornell University risk assessment specialists.
6 The University of the Aristide Foundation is Haiti's largest medical school. It opened in 2001 and moved to a newly constructed campus in 2003.

References

Board, T. E. (2019, November 5). Haiti's Ashes. *The New York Times*. www.nytimes.com/2019/11/04/opinion/haiti-protests.html?searchResultPosition=1

Degraff, M. (2022, October 14). As a child in Haiti, I was taught to despise my language and myself. *The New York Times*. www.nytimes.com/2022/10/14/opinion/haiti-kreyol-creole-language-education.html

1 A Concise History of Community Engagement in Higher Education

Planning and leading a community-engaged performance tour requires a working understanding of service-learning, community engagement, and engaged scholarship. This chapter defines those terms, contextualizes them within the development of higher education in Europe and the U.S., and traces their adoption in U.S. colleges and universities.

Let us begin with the concept of gentility. (This may seem a random topic, but I ask the reader to stick with me for a moment.) Gentility was a central tenet of the 18th-century European noble class and referred in a general sense to the characteristics, manners, and attitudes of those surrounded by some level of culture, wealth, and privilege. Gentility was fundamental in the development of higher education in Europe, which, in the early modern era, became more aristocratic and guided by a social rationale of educating the elite (Carpentier, 2019, p. x). American colonial colleges in the 18th century generally reflected their European heritage and aspired to provide a liberal education for young white men who aspired to become gentlemen. A gentleman "knew Latin and Greek but also how to dance gracefully. Acquiring the wealth to maintain the lifestyle of a gentleman was a separate—and essential—matter" (Geiger, 2016, p. 155). Colleges catered to a narrow social base—primarily the Northeastern elite class—and sought to inculcate the virtues, manners, and education required to assume a respected societal position. Campuses represented a path to maintaining or earning social status, supported primarily by affluent, educated patrons.

Nineteenth-century U.S. society identified two distinct classes: the professional class "whose proper business is to teach the true principles of religion, law, medicine, science, art, and literature" and the significantly larger industrial class, which "engaged in some form of labor in agriculture, commerce, and the arts" (Turner, 1851, p. 1). Those desiring to expand access to the industrial class argued that the classical course in colleges catered to an elite student population and was "unsuited to the needs of an industrial and agricultural community" (Becker, 1943, p. 20). This position was not without merit; there were many barriers to gaining access to higher education, which reflected contemporary societal norms and attitudes regarding socioeconomics, gender, and race. For example, entrance exams required basic knowledge of Latin and Greek, acquired primarily at grammar schools and academies predominately located in the Northeast (Geiger, p. 155). Ninety percent of the population resided on farms in rural settings. To obtain more than a rudimentary education in the first half of the 19th century in the United States, one needed to be a white male living in an urban—primarily northeastern—area and have the means to attend school and absorb the expense of living away from home. As a result, much of the U.S. populace in the early 19th century perceived higher education as inherently undemocratic (Becker, p. 20). These circumstances set the stage for sweeping legislation revolutionizing higher education: the Morrill Land Grant Acts.

The Morrill Land Grant Acts

Frequent political instability across Europe in the 19th century had far-reaching implications on higher educational institutions, the chief among them was the development or reinforcement of distinct national educational models, most notably in England, France, and Germany. While different, the three nations shared a common approach—dividing knowledge into disciplines and developing a specialized faculty. This new type of institution developed independently throughout Europe and, with particular influence from the German model, evolved into the modern research-oriented university. Simultaneously, the second industrial revolution (1870–1914) initiated technological innovations requiring specialized workers in fields such as chemistry and electricity. As nations competed for innovation and production, universities became inextricably linked to the furtherance of national interests.

The need for an educated workforce, combined with other factors, including broadening colonization and economic crises, stimulated interest in the democratization of higher education. New universities began meeting new technical and industrial needs while fostering higher social status for the working class. While limited in scope, two notable examples were the University Extension in the U.K. from the 1870s onward and the *Universités Populaires* in France from 1899.

As championed by Vermont Senator Justin Morrill and signed into law by President Abraham Lincoln, the Agricultural College Act of 1862 (known today as the Morrill Land Grant Act) was considerably more extensive and transformational than its European counterparts. Each participating state was granted 30,000 acres of federal land for each representative and senator in Congress, with the stipulation that the land was to be used to create an endowment to support at least one college that promoted practical subjects, such as agriculture and mechanic arts (the emerging field of engineering quickly displaced mechanic arts), without excluding scientific and classical studies. The act fundamentally altered the nature of U.S. higher education, which ultimately drove societal change by fostering broader access, institutionalizing practical studies and integrating them with liberal education, and establishing a foundation for making a more expansive higher education scope possible (Whalen, 2002, p. 1). The legacy of the Morrill Act was "the accessible state college and university, characterized by a curriculum that was broad and utilitarian" (Thelin, 2011, p. 76).

Historians have long praised the Morrill Act as the foundation of a "linear, evolutionary march of democratic progress, where the common man achieves increasing access to the power centers of society" (Sorber, 2018, p. 7). Present-day colleges and universities often point to the Morrill Act as a high point in higher education innovation, and advocates of community engagement in academe argue that its centrality is perhaps most germane for public and land-grant institutions (Fitzgerald et al., 2012, p. 8).[1]

Several historians have reassessed some of the democratic ideals attributed to the Morrill Act. While acknowledging that early land-grant colleges reflected the country's racial and social climate of the time, Sorber has noted that the ideas behind the legislation "were tied to socially constructed, class-based images of white manhood, and female and African American students had to create or 'negotiate' their own land-grant purposes and spaces," and that the act "perpetuated dominant values and knowledge" (2018, p. 4). Indeed, the U.S. was land rich but cash poor, and the elite could not finance a noble lifestyle with plentiful land alone. The founders envisaged a future where personal enrichment and the public good were inextricably tied together. Commerce, expansion, and innovation were necessary to realize this future, and they understood that a large-scale overhaul of the education system would be instrumental in bringing these efforts to fruition.

The second Morrill Act of 1890 sought to provide educational opportunities for formerly enslaved people and targeted former Confederate states by forbidding racial discrimination by institutions if they received federal funds. However, a state could evade the provision by maintaining a separate land-grant institution for African Americans and supporting it with an "equitable" division of funds. States often interpreted "equitable" as being less than equal or proportionate, and "inadequate funds and resources were common threads which ran through each of the colleges" well into the 20th century (Humphries, 1991, p. 5). Thus, this is how the federal government granted tacit approval of a separate-but-equal standard that emerged in higher education six years before the *Plessy v. Ferguson* decision.

While not excluded from taking advantage of the advances in higher education, female college admission remained low. For those who attended, college admission "hardly precluded segregation within the walls" (Thelin, p. 98). By 1860, at least 45 institutions with names ranging from "college" to "female seminary" offered degrees to women. Following the Civil War, coeducation for women and men gained currency, but women were mistreated and prevented from having the same experiences as their male colleagues. While unfortunate in coeducational institutions, this generated the setting for women's colleges such as Bryn Mawr, Smith, and Vassar to flourish. Women's access to education also gained momentum in Europe, with movements beginning in Switzerland, Sweden, and the U.K. in the second half of the 19th century (Carpentier, 2019).

Colleges funded by the Morrill Act also emerged at the expense of indigenous populations and lands.[2] As the country continued to acquire lands to the west through the Louisiana Purchase and the Mexican War, leaders began speaking of the country's "manifest destiny" to reach the Pacific Ocean. Overall, the government took possession of nearly two billion acres of land by entering into coerced, unfair, or unratified treaties, purchasing land for unfairly low prices, or seizing property. Nearly 80,000 parcels amassed through seizure or treaties were granted through the Morrill Act (Lee & Ahtone, 2020). Through that lens, the Morrill Act "can be seen as one state-sponsored mechanism of both literally and symbolically establishing settler colonialism" (Nash, 2019, p. 448).[3]

Institutions that benefited from land appropriated from indigenous communities have begun to revise their narratives and wrestle with an appropriate way to recognize the circumstances that led to their founding. One such approach is an acknowledgment statement, such as that of Cornell University.

> Cornell University is located on the traditional homelands of the Gayogo̱hó:nǫ' (the Cayuga Nation). The Gayogo̱hó:nǫ' are members of the Haudenosaunee Confederacy, an alliance of six sovereign Nations with a historic and contemporary presence on this land. The Confederacy precedes the establishment of Cornell University, New York State, and the United States of America. We acknowledge the painful history of Gayogo̱hó:nǫ' dispossession, and honor the ongoing connection of Gayogo̱hó:nǫ' people, past and present, to these lands and waters.
> (Cornell University, 2021)

"The United States have achieved many great things, but it also has a complex history with dark and cruel periods, including the mistreatment of Native Americans and the taking of a great deal of their land," begins the Association of Public & Land-Grant Universities land acknowledgment statement. "While we cannot change the past, public and land-grant universities have and will be focused on building a better future for everyone" (2022).

The Modern University

In the early 20th century, American institutions sought to codify academic standards, attract graduate students, and adopt the paradigmatic German model in which the primary feature is a focus on specialized disciples. These disciplines began supplanting classical courses, professional organizations grew around them, and private foundations began to fund related institutional initiatives. Despite notable advances, academe still catered to the elite; by the late 1930s, much of the public recognized faculty as experts in increasingly esoteric fields. Higher education began to be labeled by critics as an "ivory tower"—aloof, pretentious, and disengaged (Shapin, 2012, p. 14). According to Thelin (p. 222), "Professors possessed expertise, as documented by their holding of a Ph.D., but . . . their pull was inward. The university was a citadel or haven, not a publicly-minded entity."

World War II initiated a period of conflict, destruction, and hardship previously unseen by the global population. When the U.S. entered the war in 1941, universities became instruments of the war effort, supplying the military with practical knowledge, materials, and trained personnel. Research universities became valuable resources for national defense and essential players in the new era of "big science." President Dwight D. Eisenhower famously warned the country in his 1961 farewell address about the growing power of the "military-industrial complex." Senator J. William Fulbright expanded upon Eisenhower's warning by his characterization of the "military-industrial-academic complex" (Leslie, 1993). After the war, research universities' practices profoundly influenced U.S. academic culture, stimulating greater competition, diversity of practices and disciplines, and knowledge creation. During that same time, the GI Bill generated a significant enrollment increase and brought millions of first-generation students to college, along with their cultural trappings. As colleges and universities served larger percentages of the population, states met the sharply increased demand by creating flagship, regional, and community institutions. In the mid-20th century, U.S. higher education entered an unprecedented age of expansion and solidification while obtaining global prominence.

The post-World War II years solidified three now-ubiquitous higher education missions: teaching, research, and service. People of all social strata became engaged in an ideological battle between capitalism and communism, and a struggle to instill and expand democratic and progressive ideals around access and inclusivity. Politics and education became entangled, and educational institutions played a pivotal role in national interests. Today's college and university systems are the direct results of this post-war era.

Service-Learning

The zeitgeist of the 1960s included a growing awareness of social justice, isolated or underserved populations, decolonization, and globalization. In both the U.S. and Europe, the university no longer catered to an elite population and became open to all qualified students. (In practice, however, significant barriers to enrollment continued to exist.) At the same time, high-profile governmental initiatives focused on social justice; notable examples include President John F. Kennedy's founding of the Peace Corps in 1961 and the origination of the idea for the Volunteers in Service to America (known today as the AmeriCorps programs), which the Lyndon Johnson administration launched in 1965. College and university campuses channeled this spirit by establishing programs to attract historically marginalized students and embracing volunteerism to engage with local communities. Such programs were initially limited to extracurricular organizations. As one example, students worked under the auspices of the national University Year for ACTION program, which involved more than 10,000 volunteers from 100 campuses in service programs throughout the 1970s (Kendall, 1990, p. 8).

These changes resulted in the foundation of a new movement aiming to bridge the gap between service and education. The term *service-learning* was coined in 1967 and grew out of Robert Sigmon and William Ramsey's work at the Southern Regional Education Board (Eyler & Giles, 1999, p. 78). The term gained traction, and in 1979, the National Center for Service-Learning emerged from the National Student Volunteer Program, which began in 1969. Service-learning gained a foothold on campuses through extracurricular volunteer programs; however, these programs remained outside sponsoring institutions' missions and curricula (Kendall, p. 13). While beneficial, volunteerism is predicated on the idea that a more equipped person or group assists a less equipped person or group. Such a perspective has limited viability within academic disciplines because it can foster either implicit or explicit paternalistic and non-democratic relationships between the servers and the served. Moreover, volunteerism typically does not include a reflection component for the servers or the served. Without this vital element, volunteer experiences may not elicit the most lasting educational benefit for the participants.

In the late 1970s and 1980s, a materialistic shift in U.S. culture exacerbated by the U.S. economic downturn further weakened the nascent service-learning movement. University students became more interested in their diplomas' economic value and less committed to gaining knowledge to serve the public good (Astin, 1998, p. 132). This pivot partially explains why many students chose pre-professional degrees and technical training over liberal arts (Breneman, 1994, p. 9). The relationship between the college student and the institution became increasingly transactional, with the degree as a gateway to personal advancement and financial reward.

Many campuses returned to initiatives grounded in volunteerism to counter this shift in student culture, and service-learning was temporarily lost in the mix. However, volunteerism has always been largely disassociated from the curriculum for the aforementioned reasons. As universities analyzed their volunteer programs, they began to turn to newer models, and service-learning once again had a chance to develop. In the late 1980s, members of Campus Compact[4] and the National Society for Experiential Education (NSEE) began to incorporate community engagement into colleges' and universities' core missions. This led to NSEE's publication of ten principles combining service and learning, guided by the philosophy that "service, combined with learning, adds value to each and transforms both" (Honnet & Poulsen, 1989, p. 1). The principles deemphasized volunteerism in favor of reciprocal partnerships with the community and a democratic approach to information sharing. The authors asserted that service-learning clarifies community service and academic content while enabling faculty to draw pedagogical connections between course material and service experiences. Robert Sigmon's service and learning typology chart illustrates this another way (1994, p. 1).

- service-LEARNING: learning goals are emphasized.
- SERVICE-learning: service outcomes are emphasized.
- service learning: service and learning goals are separate.
- SERVICE-LEARNING: service and learning are emphasized equally.

Contemporary scholars define service-learning as "a form of experiential education in which students engage in activities that address human and community needs, together with structured opportunities for reflection designed to achieve desired learning outcomes" (Jacoby, 2015, p. 2). The term focuses on the "particular potential for and the critical importance of the *integration* of service and learning" (Kendall, 1990, p. 24), and according to Jacoby, the hyphen joining the two words "symbolizes reflection and depicts the symbiotic relationship between service and learning" (p. 2).[5] Some scholars hone this definition by contextualizing service-learning within academia:

> Service-learning [is] a course-based, credit-bearing, educational experience in which students (a) participate in an organized service activity that meets identified community needs and (b) reflect on the service activity in such a way as to gain further understanding of course content, a broader appreciation of the discipline, and an enhanced sense of civic responsibility.
> (Bringle & Hatcher, 1995, p. 112)

Practitioners can create more nuanced service-learning applications by conceptualizing and defining them as a program, a philosophy, or a pedagogy. As a program, service-learning focuses on completing tasks chosen in combination with learning goals and designed to meet community needs (Kendall, 1990, p. 20). As a philosophy, service-learning is designed to "move from charity to justice, from service to the elimination of need" (Jacoby, 2015, pp. 4–5) and emphasizes active engagement, reciprocity, and "mutuality in learning between the student and the community" (Kendall, 1990, p. 23). As a pedagogy, service-learning is governed by the principle that learning does not necessarily occur as a result of experience but through experiential learning and conscious reflection.

Reciprocity and a democratic, i.e., equitable and equal, relationship between the institution and the community are cornerstones of service-learning. "Both the server and those served teach, and both learn" (p. 22). Students conceptualize their service-learning experience as working *with* someone instead of *for* them, and practitioners design experiences "*with* the community to meet needs identified *by* the community" (Jacoby, 2015, p. 4). Additionally (but of equal importance), reciprocal campus–community partnerships can counteract the academy's frequently perceived exclusionary and elitist culture.

Due to this emphasis on reciprocity, the term service-learning passed out of vogue in some circles. The word *service* implies a hierarchical, as opposed to mutual relationship between the servers and the served, and suggests that the former population does something *to* the community instead of *with* it. For this reason, "service-learning" is often termed "community-based education" and "engaged learning."

Engaged Scholarship and Community Engagement

In the 1990s, a new body of scholarship emerged around Ernest Boyer's seminal works: *Scholarship Reconsidered* (1990) and *The Scholarship of Engagement* (1996). Boyer asserts that through sweeping changes such as the Land Grant Act and the GI Bill, colleges and universities have historically been linked to American culture and committed to the common good. He urges the academy to "become a more vigorous partner in the search for answers to our most pressing social, civic, economic, and moral problems" and to look beyond the traditional faculty responsibilities of teaching, research, and service. Boyer's *scholarship of engagement* shuns a narrow definition of research as the only legitimate path to creating knowledge and regards service as scholarship when it requires the application of disciplinary expertise. This integrative approach to traditional faculty roles has become known as *community-engaged scholarship*. In 2008, the *Imagining America Tenure Team* expanded that definition:

> Publicly engaged academic work is scholarly or creative activity integral to a faculty member's academic area. It encompasses different forms of making knowledge about, for, and with diverse publics and communities. Through a coherent, purposeful sequence of activities, it contributes to the public good and yields artifacts of public and intellectual value.
> (Ellison & Eatman, 2008, p. 6)

Furthering this definition, community engagement can be defined as

> the collaboration between institutions of higher education and their larger communities (local, regional/state, national, global) for the mutually beneficial exchange of knowledge and resources in a context of partnership and reciprocity.
> (Driscoll, 2008, p. 39)

By the late 1990s, most U.S. campuses had some support for faculty interested in creating engaging course content and establishing community partnerships (Saltmarsh & Hartley, 2017, p. 116). The 1990s also saw the founding of academic journals devoted to community-based research, the first of which was the *Michigan Journal of Community Service Learning* (University of Michigan). Stemming from a 1998 conference, Campus Compact published *Benchmarks for Campus/Community Partnerships* (listed in Chapter 3), which presented essential components of democratic partnerships and strategies for sustaining and integrating the partnerships with the missions of partnering institutions (Torres, 2000, p. 5).

The first years of the 21st century marked increased efforts to bring community engagement and service-learning from the margins to mainstream higher education. In 2012, the National Task Force on Civic Learning and Democratic Engagement, sponsored by the American Association of Colleges & Universities and the U.S. Department of Education, published *A Crucible Moment: College Learning and Democracy's Future*. The report asserted that "opportunities for civic learning and democratic engagement remain optional rather than expected on most campuses, and peripheral to the perceived 'real' academic mission" and advocated for a ground-up reinvention of the mission of higher education (National Task Force, 2012, p. 41). Many campuses subsequently added language regarding service-learning or community engagement to their mission statements and established offices to support related initiatives.

Institutions also began to codify a new approach to civic and community engagement consisting of four primary features. First, engaged academic work gained recognition as a viable means of fulfilling institutions' research and education missions. (This was particularly true for land-grant universities aiming to connect with the Morrill Acts' democratic ideals.) The second change was that institutions began to view external entities as equal partners in engagement initiatives. As defined by the Kellogg Commission in 1999:

> Engagement goes well beyond extension, conventional outreach, and even most conceptions of public service. Inherited concepts emphasize a one-way process in which the university transfers its expertise to key constituents. Embedded in the engagement ideal is a commitment to sharing and reciprocity.

Third, the focus of engagement work shifted from isolated projects supported by a limited funding source to long-term community partnerships encompassing a series of projects that "operate synergistically and through broad participation so that all are working toward a common set of goals" (Bruininks et al., 2014, p. 157). The fourth distinction is arguably the most significant: institutions began to pivot from merely conducting engagement initiatives to using public engagement as a strategy for "accomplishing important institutional priorities and facilitating institutional transformation and advancement" (p. 157).

Successful community engagement work requires a commitment from a diverse group of individuals, including administrators, faculty, and support staff. Firm and equal commitment often remain elusive. Concerns range from the expense of starting and maintaining community partnerships to the possibility that engagement initiatives will detract from traditional disciplinary scholarship to fears that institutions will not recognize engagement work as worthy of institutional rewards (p. 172). Administrators, scholars, and practitioners seeking to create institutional change around community engagement envisage a continuum with traditional scholarship at one end and community-engaged, reciprocal scholarship at the other (Ellison & Eatman, 2008, p. ix). These authors advocated for equal value and shared assessment standards regardless of one's place on the continuum. "For the publicly engaged faculty member, tenure review should mark the point where the results of public and community-based inquiry are accorded the full dignity of informed peer review" (p. xi). For this to occur, engaged scholarship must be integrated into the core teaching, research, and service missions of the institution, and scholarship should "embrace both the act of engaging (bringing campuses and communities together) and the product of engagement (the spread of scholarship-focused, evidence-based practices in communities)" (Fitzgerald et al., 2012, p. 13).

Today's colleges and universities have provided unparalleled access to higher education, and U.S. campuses are more diverse than ever. However, they continue to reflect the national culture's biases and prejudices. They cater to and create a social elite and perpetuate distinctions based on social constructs. This harkens back to "the gentleman ideal of the mid-19th century or the preoccupation with social rank in colonial and Federalist society" (Geiger, 2015, p. 989). Critics of the higher education system argue that it has perpetuated a caste system since its inception: The dominant caste—white males—has retained control of the system, which disadvantages lower castes through legacy strictures based on race, gender, and class (Patton, 2016, p. 318). In summary, higher education continues to struggle with many of the same social and cultural challenges that plagued its formative years.

Against that backdrop, today's growing emphasis on purposeful community engagement in academe may be viewed as a historical corrective. This represents a watershed opportunity for ensemble directors. By definition, performance tours occur off-campus. The products associated with tours, e.g., public concerts, are socially produced; they are presented by a group of people for a group of people. Indeed, music is primarily social and is generally composed and performed for others. Traditional ensemble performance tours focus primarily on performance and tourism, whereas community-engaged performance tours place performance and community engagement on equal footing. These tours allow students to take social interaction a significant step further by engaging *with* communities rather than performing *for* them. By combining musical, cultural, and societal goals and learning outcomes, educators can summon their students' collective potential to create positive change.

Notes

1 The Morrill Act was inspired by another social agenda. Most European universities traced their origins back to a nation's prevalent religion, hence the Latin and Greek theology. However, many of the most notable founders of the United States lacked strong adherence to established religion, which was viewed (alongside the state) as an oppressor of people. Early U.S. leaders desired to be separate from any remote British authority, which had been tightening its grip on their lives (although their liberties far exceeded those of their fellow citizens in Britain).
2 As of this writing, American Indian, Indian, indigenous peoples, and native American are used interchangeably in current literature. The word *tribe* is considered derogatory in Canada but acceptable in the U.S. (Diamond, 2008, p. 4). Christopher Columbus thought he had landed in the Indies (as China, Japan, and India were then known in Europe), and native inhabitants of the New World came to be called Indians. The term American Indian dates to 1507 when the German cartographer Martin Waldseemüller published the first map that used the term America in honor of the Italian explorer Amerigo Vespucci. The term Native American was adopted in the 1960s to separate from colonial associations.
3 *Settler colonialism* refers to the assumption of land with the intention of staying permanently. This differs from *exploitative colonialism*, where land and existing inhabitants are exploited for resources and labor (Veracini, 2010, p. 8).
4 Campus Compact, a coalition of university presidents founded in 1985, began with an overarching mission to foster democracy by promoting civic engagement in higher education. The coalition currently includes nearly 1,100 colleges and universities across the globe.
5 That definition notwithstanding, some scholars and institutions eschew the hyphen.

References

Association of Public & Land-Grant Universities. (n.d.). *Statement of Land Acknowledgment*. https://www.aplu.org/about-us/land-acknowledgment/

Astin, A. W. (1998). The changing American college student: Thirty-year trends, 1966–1996. *Review of Higher Education, 21*(2), 115–135.

Becker, C. L. (1943). *Cornell university: Founders and the founding*. Cornell University Press.

Boyer, E. L. (1990). *Scholarship reconsidered: priorities of the professoriate*. Princeton, N.J.: The Carnegie Foundation for the Advancement of Teaching.

Boyer, E. L. (1996). The Scholarship of Engagement. *Bulletin of the American Academy of Arts and Sciences, 49*(7), 18–33. https://doi.org/10.2307/3824459

Breneman, D. W. (1994). *Liberal arts colleges: Thriving, surviving, or endangered?* Brookings Institution.

Bringle, R. G., & Hatcher, J. A. (1995). A service-learning curriculum for faculty. *Michigan Journal of Community Service Learning, 2*(1), 112–122.

Bruininks, R., Furko, A., Sommers, J., Konkle, E. A., & Jones, R. (2014). Institutionalizing civic engagement at the University of Minnesota. In H. Boyle (Ed.), *Democracy's education: Public work, citizenship, and the future of colleges and universities* (pp. 80–90). Vanderbilt University Press.

Carpentier, V. (2019). The history of higher education in modern Europe. In J. L. Rury & E. H. Tamura (Eds.), *The Oxford handbook of the history of education* (pp. 216–27). Oxford University Press.

Cornell University American Indian and Indigenous Studies Program. (2021). *Land acknowledgment*. https://cals.cornell.edu/american-indian-indigenous-studies/about/land-acknowledgment

Diamond, B. (2008). *Native American music in eastern North America: Experiencing music, expressing culture*. Oxford University Press.

Driscoll, A. (2008). Carnegie's community-engagement classification: intentions and insights. Change: *The Magazine of Higher Learning, 40*(1), 38–41.

Ellison, J. K., & Eatman, T. (2008). *Scholarship in public: Knowledge creation and tenure policy in the engaged university: A resource on promotion and tenure in the arts, humanities, and design*. Imagining America. https://surface.syr.edu/ia/16

Eyler, J., & Giles, D. (1999). *Where's the learning in service learning?* Jossey-Bass.

Fitzgerald, H., Bruns, K., Sonka, S., Furco, A., & Swanson, L. (2012). The centrality of engagement in higher education. *Journal of Higher Education Outreach and Engagement, 16*(3), 7–29.

Geiger, R. L. (2015). *The history of American higher education: Learning and culture from the founding to World War II*. Princeton University Press.

Honnet, E. P., Poulsen, S. J., & Johnson Foundation (Racine, Wis.). (1989). *Principles of good practice for combining service and learning*. Johnson Foundation.

Humphries, F. (1991). 1890 land-grant institutions: Their struggle for survival and equality. *Agricultural History, 65*(2), 3–11. www.jstor.org/stable/3743704

Jacoby, B. (2015). *Service-learning essentials: Questions, answers, and lessons learned*. Jossey-Bass.

Kendall, J. C. (1990). *Combining service and learning: A resource book for community and public service*. National Society for Internships and Experiential Education.

Lee, R., & Ahtone, T. (2020, March 30). Land-grab universities. *High Country News*. www.hcn.org/issues/52.4/indigenous-affairs-education-land-grab-universities/print_view

Leslie, S. W. (1993). *The cold war and American science: The military-industrial-academic complex at MIT and Stanford*. Columbia University Press.

Nash, M. (2019). Entangled pasts: Land-grant colleges and American Indian dispossession. *History of Education Quarterly, 59*(4), 437–467. doi:10.1017/heq.2019.31

National Task Force on Civic Learning and Democratic Engagement and Association of American Colleges and Universities. (2012). *A crucible moment: College learning & democracy's future*. Association of American Colleges and Universities. www.aacu.org/sites/default/files/files/crucible/Crucible_508F.pdf

Patton, L. D. (2016). Disrupting postsecondary prose: toward a critical race theory of higher education. *Urban Education, 51*(3), 315–342. https://doi.org/10.1177/0042085915602542

Saltmarsh, J., & Hartley, M. (2017). A brief history of the civic engagement movement in American higher education. In T. D. Mitchell & T. K. Eatman (Eds.), *The Cambridge handbook of service learning and community engagement* (pp. 112–124). doi:10.1017/9781316650011.012

Shapin, S. (2012). The ivory tower: The history of a figure of speech and its cultural uses. *British Journal for the History of Science, 45*(1), 1–27. doi:10.1017/S0007087412000118

Sigmon, R., & Council of Independent Colleges. (1994). *Linking service with learning : a report from cic*. Council of Independent Colleges.
Sorber, N. M. (2018). *Land-grant colleges and popular revolt: The origins of the Morrill Act and the reform of higher education*. Cornell University Press.
Thelin, J. R. (2011). *A history of American higher education* (2nd ed.). Johns Hopkins University Press.
Torres, J. (Ed.). (2000). *Benchmarks for campus/community partnerships*. Campus Compact.
Turner, J. (1851). *A plan for an industrial university for the state of Illinois: Submitted to the farmers' convention at Granville, held November 18, 1851*. (n.p.)
University Mission. (n.d.). Cornell University. www.cornell.edu/about/mission.cfm
Veracini, L. (2010). *Settler colonialism: A theoretical overview*. Palgrave Macmillan.
Whalen, M. (2002). *A land-grant university*. Cornell University 2001–02 Financial Plan. https://dpb.cornell.edu/documents/1000046.pdf

2 Traditional and Community-Engaged Performance Tours
From Tourism to Partnership

Why Tour?

In addition to on-campus rehearsals and performances, ensemble directors in academic institutions routinely engage in local, regional, and international tours. Touring is often woven into the ensemble experience, and students who participate do so with the expectation that they will tour regularly. Given the ubiquity of ensemble tours, remarkably little research has been conducted in this area, even as an entire industry of performance tour companies has grown around it. Why do ensembles travel? Why do ensemble directors go to the trouble and expense of touring, especially when their efforts rarely receive additional remuneration or a reduced teaching load? The answers to these questions are related to goals associated with the music curriculum and extracurricular learning goals. This chapter begins by exploring these motivations and continues with an examination of traditional and community-engaged performance tours and their relationship to tourism.

The curricular benefits of touring have been the subject of only a few peer-reviewed empirical studies (Helsel, 2015, p. 3). In my experience, directors choose to tour for various curricular reasons, including, though not limited to, the following:

- The tour represents a musical goal of performing for off-campus audiences, which, as a capstone project, motivates students to perform at a high level.
- Performances in prestigious venues inspire students by cultivating the impression of importance and exclusivity, and drawing a thread between historically important artists and current performances.
- If the tour includes multiple performances, students hone their professionalism by learning to produce high-quality music regardless of the many unpredictable variables associated with touring, from truncated warm-up routines to perform in various halls and acoustic environments for different audiences.

DOI: 10.4324/9781003278696-3

- Depending on the tour location, students may become more informed musical interpreters by performing in historically significant venues or becoming more aware of a composer's background and culture.
- Some directors frame tours around competitions, professional conventions, or festivals. In all cases, students are motivated by the prospect of critical feedback and often measure their music-making quality against peer ensembles.
- Performing for younger or less experienced musicians often inspires students, for example, when a university ensemble performs at a high school.
- Combined performances with local ensembles, especially if professional or semiprofessional musicians are involved, expose students to a level of performance they may not experience in their home institution. Moreover, these performances, as when an academic choir collaborates with a local orchestra, may enable students to perform repertoire not possible at home.

All these cases focus on inspiring students to make music at their highest level. Depending on tour frequency, directors may leverage tours toward a higher level of musicianship throughout the academic year, transcending the tour as a capstone project and fostering long-term musical growth measurable through qualitative assessment of rehearsal culture and concert performances.

The extracurricular benefits of touring typically include basic personal development, such as self-confidence, adaptability, and cross-cultural competencies. To some degree, all travel is educational as it broadens the mind as people learn from and interpret experiences (Stone & Petrick, 2013, p. 731). However, there is a paucity of research on travel's formal educational benefits (Falk et al., 2012). Moreover, it is difficult to determine what constitutes cultural learning, let alone assess its value. Ritchie et al. (2003) opined that the concept of educative travel is a broad and complicated area, which explains why "tourism academics and industry have to date largely ignored this field" (p. 9).

Most research on cultural outcomes associated with traveling focuses on young adults and college students engaged in international study abroad experiences, which have been studied extensively since 1990. Relevant peer-reviewed studies across various disciplines focus primarily on undergraduate students studying at universities in foreign countries (Stone & Petrick, p. 735).

Researchers have shown that study abroad experiences can require students to exercise flexibility and adaptability by adjusting to predetermined schedules, communicating with unfamiliar people, and, even on a basic level, adapting to local practices and unfamiliar systems. Indeed, students frequently learn essential information about the local culture, communicate with hosts, ask basic questions and understand responses in a foreign language, employ nonverbal communication, and manage stressors ranging from new observations to unfamiliar foods and uncomfortable climates. This can foster a variety of basic skills associated with personal development, including confidence and self-reliance (Gmelch, 1997), problem-solving, interpersonal skills

(Pearce & Foster, 2007), time management, and communication (Scarinci & Pearce, 2012).

Most studies cite cultural competencies—also called intercultural and cross-cultural competencies in the literature—as a primary educative benefit of study abroad experiences. Before listing them, the terms *culture* and *cultural competency* require definition. According to UNESCO, culture is

> the set of distinctive spiritual, material, intellectual, and emotional features of a society or social group, encompassing all the ways of being in that society; at a minimum, including art and literature, lifestyles, ways of living together, value systems, traditions, and beliefs.
>
> (UNESCO, 2010)

Each culture is the sum of its members' beliefs and practices and is distinguished most easily from another culture by comparing and contrasting those practices. Individuals of a culture are not easily divisible (Deardorff, 2020, p. 4).

Many definitions and terms are associated with cultural competencies. Deardorff writes that cultural competencies are "in essence . . . about improving human interactions across difference, whether within a society (differences due to age, gender, religion, socioeconomic status, political affiliation, ethnicity, and so on) or across borders" (p. 5). UNESCO lists respect, self-awareness, empathy with other perspectives and worldviews, listening, adaptation, relationship building, and cultural humility among the markers of cultural competency (2013, p. 24). Individuals build cultural competency by acquiring "adequate knowledge about particular cultures, as well as general knowledge about . . . issues arising when members of different cultures interact, holding receptive attitudes that encourage establishing and maintaining contact with diverse others," and developing the skills required to interact with others from different cultures (p. 16).

Researchers studying abroad have found that students develop a more complex cultural view (Janes, 2008), enhanced cross-cultural competence (Laubscher, 1994), greater empathy for the viewpoints of other nations (Carlson & Widaman, 1988), and a lasting impact on their worldview (Dwyer, 2004). It is worth noting that extant studies of travel learning focus on international, as opposed to domestic, experiences (Stone & Petrick, 2013). While it is difficult to imagine that domestic travel offers comparable cross-cultural experiences, other important learning outcomes may result.

Traditional performance tours differ from study abroad experiences in many respects, including duration, scope, and mission; students studying abroad typically have much more individual freedom and leisure time to explore the local culture. These differences notwithstanding, we can glean valuable information from these studies. Whether traveling on a performance tour or studying abroad, curricular concepts are rarely students' only learning outcomes.

Tourism and Education

According to the World Tourism Organization (2008), a *visitor* is someone who travels outside their accustomed environment for less than a year for any purpose other than employment by a resident in the country, or places visited. These trips qualify as tourism, and tourism refers to visitors' activity. By extension, we must examine tourism when determining the educational benefits of ensemble performance tours.

Modern tourism is primarily a Western concept that stems from the *grand tour* of the 17th century, which was a traditional rite of passage for affluent young European men seeking to enhance their education and broaden their worldview. With the industrial revolution and the advent of rail travel in the 19th century, the grand tour gradually morphed into a status symbol for upper-class students from Europe, the U.K., and the U.S. These students traveled abroad to learn languages and examine the roots of Western civilizations through art, culture, and language. Throughout the 20th century, economic prosperity led more people to acquire expendable income, earn frequent work holidays, and take advantage of the increased flexibility afforded by automobile and air travel. The growing population of travelers led to a new supply of seaside resorts in Europe and the United Kingdom, tropical resorts in numerous global locations, and amusement and theme parks in the U.K. and North America (Falk et al., 2012, p. 910). Before the end of the 20th century, tourism grew into the world's largest and most important industry (Gibson & Connell, 2005, p. 7) and an essential element of globalization (selfie, p. 22). In the Internet age, the boundary between everyday life and tourism has become increasingly blurred (Falk et al., 2012, p. 910). This was especially true during the COVID-19 (coronavirus) pandemic, as media and communication technologies capitalized on the ubiquity of tourism and created "virtual" excursions. Those developments notwithstanding, tourism's centrality was evident during the pandemic when people stopped traveling, and dependent industries ranging from airlines to restaurants suffered from dire financial straits.

Tourists gather knowledge as they "understand, learn, discover, explore, and make sense of other places" (Casella, 1997, p. 52). Tourism's concentrated engagement with unfamiliar cultures "lends its subjects a mantle of cosmopolite authority that years of classroom instruction rarely approach" (Werry, 2008, p. 18). Indeed, Dierking (2005, p. 146) suggests that a new tourism model centered on learning about history and culture and fostering a broader knowledge-based worldview has overtaken the archetypal 20th-century Western vacation with sandy beaches or roller coasters. In that respect, the educational ideal of the *grand tour* has come full circle.

Experiential learning theory provides one explanation for how people learn through tourism. John Dewey believed education must be based on experience to achieve the intended benefits for teachers and learners. He proposed that experience is educational if it satisfies two principles: continuity and interaction. The learner's experiences are integrated with and influence future experiences and decisions. The learner interacts with the materials learned through reflective thinking (Dewey, 1938, pp. 35, 42, 79). Boydell (1976) defined experiential learning as "meaningful discovery" (p. 19), occurring through perceptual experiences and insight, usually resulting from personal experience.

Neo-Deweyian David Kolb expanded on this research with the following four-stage iterative cycle of experiential learning (1984), which I have adapted from a tourist's perspective.

- Learning begins with a *Concrete Experience*, an engagement with an unfamiliar place and culture.
- A period of *Reflective Observation* follows an experience, during which the student attempts to understand and articulate the feelings the experience inspired.
- The period of reflection leads to *Abstract Conceptualization*, during which the student attempts to develop a theory or explanation that defines the meaning of the experience.
- Once the student has developed an explanation, they try out that theory through *Active Experimentation* to confirm or modify the theory developed in the previous stage, which leads to another concrete experience, beginning the cycle once again.

According to Kolb's experiential learning theory, "Learning is the process whereby knowledge is created through the transformation of experience" (p. 38).

Mouton (2002) notes that travel and the concrete experience of discovery provide the tourist with an avenue for both experience and reflection, thus creating learning. However, there is no guarantee that a tourist will progress through the second, third, and fourth steps of Kolb's model. With the absence of those steps, the tourist may process experiences and observations without critical inquiry and reflection or form new conclusions and judgments based on inaccurate assumptions. Research suggests, for instance, that tourists' learning experiences may reflect misconceptions that reinforce stereotypes, colonialism, or exceptionalism that privilege some groups and subjugate others (Caton & Santos 2009). According to Laxson (1991), most tourists have an ethnocentric view of visited societies and cultures. Intentionally or not, the tourist tends to observe, process, and evaluate other people's practices and cultures according to their background, reinforcing stereotypes of their home or the host culture.

Gmelch (1997) studied the behavior and daily routines of 225 American college students traveling in Europe while on a term abroad through travel logs and personal observations. He noted "little evidence that [the students] had learned much about any European culture; their observations, on the whole, seemed naïve and simplistic." Their cultural engagement was superficial, and they had little meaningful contact with local people (p. 476). The students "rushed to the great cities of Western Europe . . . where they did cultural things such as visit museums, galleries, and look at great architecture" (p. 482). However, their journals and responses reflected a shallow level of cultural competency. Gmelch does not state a reason for this, but one hypothesis is that students spent an equal or greater amount of time observing people in their ordinary surroundings and, knowingly or not, made assumptions based on their observations and informed by their cultural background. While museums and prestigious venues may constitute tourist "must-see" artistic outlets, the culture of everyday life is arguably more important. Locations and practices common in local contexts may include a significant experience for visitors; they are *experienced* and not merely observed. As Robinson and Smith write,

> tourists spend large amounts of time "walking around" and "people watching," and in the process observing and encountering aspects of the hosts' culture in the form of everyday practices and behaviors. Far from being culture proof, it is particularly these aspects of ordinary life that tourists absorb and on their return home constitute their narratives of memory of experience.
>
> (p. 27)

Inhelder and Piaget (1958) theorized that people modify their views through attempts to resolve discrepancies between existing and new information—in this context, unfamiliar cultures, practices, and surroundings. Without forming genuine relationships with members of the host population and reflecting on their experiences, it would have been surprising if the students had developed a deeper cultural understanding.

The risk of stereotype formation increases in proximity to the cultural difference separating the tourist and the local population. The tourist can reduce people to "types" or "categories" of people and perceive a reality that does not exist (MacCannell, 1984, p. 373). This most often occurs when tourists from developed countries visit less developed locations.

> Touristified ethnic groups are often weakened by a history of exploitation, limited in resources and power, and they have no big buildings, machines, monuments, or natural wonders to deflect the tourists' attention away from the intimate details of their daily lives.
>
> (p. 386)

People's cultural identity—their "otherness"—is commoditized and funneled into the global discourse of consumerism. Wood (1998) notes that ethnicity has integrated into today's climate, celebrating diversity and multiculturalism. Ethnicity has become "a signifier of something interesting to see, promote, and experience," and it is "almost a civic duty to have an ethnicity as well as to appreciate that of others" (p. 230). Smith (1978) writes that ethnic tourism is "marketed to the public in terms of quaint customs of indigenous and often exotic peoples" (p. 4). In light of this research, it is clear that tourism alone does not necessarily foster cultural competency and, in some cases, can do more harm than good.

Tourism and Traditional Performance Tours

Robinson and Smith note that tourism, broadly defined, is cultural. Tourists engage with unfamiliar cultures and places and "experience the uniqueness of each and the commonalities of all" (2006, p. 29). Defined more narrowly, *cultural tourism* refers to a tourist's

> essential motivation to discover, experience, and consume the tangible and intangible cultural attractions/products in a tourism destination. These attractions/products relate to a set of distinctive material, intellectual, spiritual and emotional features of a society that encompasses arts and architecture, historical and cultural heritage, culinary heritage, literature, music, creative industries and the living cultures with their lifestyles, value systems, beliefs and traditions.
>
> (World Tourism Organization, 2017)

Cultural tourism often trades on the consumption of history and nostalgia. There is a Western tendency to "fossilize cultures as heritage and to prioritize the built environment" (Robinson & Smith, 2006, p. 27).

Musical ensembles often select tour locations from three primary categories identified with music: *sites of creativity*, *sites of production*, and *places of performance*. Sites of creativity include internationally famous cities, locations, or structures that inspired musical creation or the homes or birthplaces of famous composers and performers. "Vivid myths of place are linked to music there, and local identity is partly constructed in relation to unique musical sounds or successful people" (Gibson & Connell, 2005, p. 43). In Salzburg, for example, tourists can visit Wolfgang Amadeus Mozart's birthplace and residence, take in a concert at the University Mozarteum, eat Mozart-branded chocolates, and enjoy a Mozart Torte in Café Tomaselli, which was Mozart's favorite coffee house. For a more diverse array of cultural attractions, travel east to Vienna, the former urban center of the Austro-Hungarian Empire, and an attractive location for many preeminent European composers, such as Beethoven, Haydn, Mozart, Schubert, and Schumann.

The second category, *sites of production*, promotes supposedly authentic places "where timeless music was made" (p. 58), such as recording studios. The third category, *places of performance*, includes historical importance and current use structures. These include venerated classical music[1] venues such as New York's Carnegie Hall or Milan's La Scala Opera House, centers of popular music such as Nashville's Grand Ole Opry or Chicago's House of Blues, and jazz clubs such as New York's Blue Note and the Village Vanguard. In many cases, ensembles can contract and rent these venues for performance, drawing a thread from admiration of past eras to present-day artistic achievement. While cultural tourism initially focused on classical music, in the latter decades of the 20th century, the revival of folk music and new nostalgia among the "baby boom" generation engendered considerable expansion and diversification of music tourism to include many genres and forms (p. 12).

An analysis of the limitations of tourism and its relationship to cultural competency appeared earlier in this chapter. Now we will examine those limits as they relate to performance tours. Tourists generally travel individually or in small groups of friends or family members. Individuals often self-select smaller cohorts to see the sights or enjoy the nightlife even in larger groups such as study abroad courses. However, a musical ensemble is a more closely-knit community for collaborative music-making. Performance tours are generally brief (from a few days to a few weeks), and students have limited time to interact with local individuals in any meaningful way. As a result, their relationship with the community will likely be inherently imbalanced. The ensemble becomes the subject (which does something), and the community is the object (which has something done to it). Therein lies a problem. While tourism may initially seem a relatively innocuous activity associated with recreation and entertainment, it can have profound economic, environmental, political, and social effects. Gibson and Connell write that tourism

> transfers capital between people and places, influences the social organization of destinations, enables the revitalization, preservation and also the destruction of cultural phenomena, and creates new landscapes. It results in the intervention of local and national governments . . . not least in the promotion of particular destinations.
>
> (p. 3)

By extension, a musical ensemble entering into an uneven or unequal relationship with a community can negatively affect both entities.

It is helpful to examine this through the lens of the highly influential philosophical essay *Ich und Du* (1923), in which the prolific Austrian philosopher and author Martin Buber (1878–1965) explores a binary definition of human relationships. For Buber, a person is constantly in dialogue with the world in one of two modes: 1) *I-You*, in which two beings meet in complete authenticity and without any qualification or objectification and 2) *I-It*, where other beings are treated as objects to be used and/or experienced. *I-You* relationships are two-sided and stimulate mutuality and reciprocity. *I-It* relationships are one-way; only one member of the relationship has agency. After being experienced, the other resides in the agent's mind, wherein the relationship is with one's self—a monologue. Buber believes the *I-It* relationship is our most familiar way of engaging with the world because it provides several practical benefits in our lives and encompasses a world of first-hand knowledge. However, it also creates an inherent separation from others.

Contemporary tourist scholars often focus on the tourist as a cocreator of meaning rather than on the tourism industry's displayed objects (Uriely, 2005). In an *I-It* relationship, the tourist returns home with memories of the trip but often without an equal, reciprocal relationship with members of the community. The following assertions of traditional American ensemble touring cultural benefits are drawn from a conversation with leaders of performance tour companies, discussed in the next section of this chapter.

- One gains deeper insight and awareness of one's culture and place in the world.
- Cultural concert tours show the world what is best about Americans and American culture.
- History comes alive when a group visits historic sites.
- Traveling to a foreign country with friends is usually an excellent trip because you can experience the ambiance of a foreign country without leaving one's social comfort zone (Gilbert, 2005, pp. 9, 37).

In my experience leading traditional performance tours, I have found these benefits to be true. Nonetheless, they all frame the ensemble as the agent in an *I-It* relationship with people and locations, however altruistic the ensemble's motives for touring may be. This describes the limited nature of most relationships between tourists and community members. There is time to develop a narrative about the hosts and their culture but insufficient time to build genuine, empathetic understanding based on shared experiences. Both tourists and hosts can create a sense of "otherness," which emerges partly from the different worldviews and stereotypes each group may have of the other (Laxson, 1991, p. 373). MacCannell notes that "any social relationship which is transitory, superficial and unequal is a primary breeding ground for deceit, exploitation, mistrust, dishonesty, and stereotype formation" (p. 388). In the early years of tourism, advocates hoped it would become a tool for improving mutual understanding between different cultures and peoples, bringing them closer together. However, one might argue that "tourism, far from bringing peoples together, has pushed them further apart because it brings out the worst in both tourists and locals" (D'Eramo, 2017, p. 89).

Tour Companies: Convenience at a Price

Ensemble directors must complete numerous extra-curricular tasks to lead a successful performance tour, including, though certainly not limited to, fundraising, accounting, and organization. For this reason, an entire industry specializing in ensemble performance tours has blossomed to support these initiatives. Thanks to these companies, today's performance tours can appear commoditized. The conductor contracts the tour company, which provides a customized tour package to a preselected destination. The conductor sometimes joins a company representative for a planning trip, and the company follows up with an itinerary, price, and cost for individual participants. If the conductor approves, the company delivers a prepackaged, curated tour, often with a representative on hand to handle logistics and liaise with tour guides on location. According to the president of a leading tour company, "We do all the design and execution ourselves. . . . To design a concert tour, one must possess knowledge of the music, the venues, the geography, the history and other areas of interest of the region being visited" (Gilbert, 2005, p. 16). Most tour companies have expertise that includes a specific region or selection of countries and hire specialists and local guides at those destinations. This assistance enables the conductor to focus on the musical aspects of the experience.

These companies frequently have established relationships with various providers and can negotiate discounted rates for bulk transportation fares and event tickets. Following are related statements from three leading tour companies: AFCEA Tour Consultants (2021), Classical Movements (2021), and Educational World Tours (2021).

> From the start, an ACFEA Tour Manager personally works with you to determine your band's musical goals, budget, size, travel dates, and itinerary. Whether you are a concert band, jazz ensemble, or a marching band, ACFEA can arrange a tour that will suit your needs.
>
> Join us to experience the finest art, music, and dance in some of our favorite international and domestic destinations, led by the Classical Movements staff you know and love. Our in-house experts will lead you from an insider's point of view and immerse you in the authentic cultural experiences of each destination, as only Classical Movements can.
>
> Educational World Tours can arrange a performance tour for your groups based on when and where you want to travel. . . . An example of the destinations available is central Europe where we can arrange for a traveling school music program to perform in Germany, Austria, and Hungary! . . . Traveling is one of the best forms of education as it allows you to interact with the world around you and broaden your horizons. While on tour students can visit famous cities such as Budapest, Salzburg, Vienna, Berlin, Munich and more.

The problem is that conveniences such as those described earlier come with a price. While tour companies greatly simplify the touring process, they also assume some level of ownership of the tour and, in effect, can lead conductors to outsource their students' educational experience, particularly concerning cultural competency.

Traditional and Community-Engaged Performance Tours 31

This section's purpose is not to disparage tour companies or persuade conductors to avoid working with them. If one chooses to hire a tour company, the key is to do so thoughtfully. Engage a company with a similar mission to yours, and set clear guidelines regarding the student's educational experience. While this will require additional time and guidance, the educational payoffs are worth it. Chapter 4 covers related pedagogy.

Tourism and Community-Engaged Performance Tours

Community-engaged performance tours are structured to begin with tourism and continue with democratic relationships with community members. Conceptually, community-engaged tours are similar to *sustainable tourism*, aiming to even the playing field between tourists and community members by considering current and future economic, social, and environmental impacts and addressing all stakeholders'[2] needs (UNWTO, 2008).[3] *Community participation* is an integral part of this concept. Community participation "implies a desire to avoid using traditional bureaucratic paternalism in which agencies believe they know what is best for people in the community" (Tosun, 2000, p. 615). It is essentially a balancing of power inspired by political theories of democracy, which posit that people have the right to be informed by and to consult with decision-makers on relevant matters (p. 614). However, participation (like democracy) is a vast concept that invites various interpretations and expectations. Furthermore, "community" itself is a tricky concept. Communities are generally defined as a group united by geography or a common characteristic. However, communities are neither discrete nor homogenous; they are heterogeneous, fluid, and complicated by internal tiers of power and privilege.

According to Pretty and Vodouhê (1995, p. 1252), the many ways that development agencies such as nongovernment organizations (NGOs) interpret and use the term *participation* exist in seven salient types. Viewing this typology through the lens of Buber's theory of human dialogue, it is only in the fifth step that the relationship moves from *I-It* to *I-You*.

1. Manipulative participation: Participation is merely a pretense. Community members have no power or agency in decisions.
2. Passive participation: People participate by being told what has happened.
3. Participation by consultation: People participate by being consulted or by answering questions. External agents define problems and information gathering, control the analysis, and do not share in decision-making.
4. Participation for material incentives: People participate by contributing resources in return for food, cash, or other material incentives. They have no stake in prolonging their efforts when the incentives end.
5. Functional participation: Such involvement may be interactive and involve shared decision-making but tends to arise only after external agents have already made significant decisions.

6. Interactive participation: Participation is a right, not just the means to achieve project goals. Groups control local decisions, determine how available resources are used, and have a stake in maintaining structures or practices.
7. Empowerment: People participate by taking initiatives independently of external institutions to change systems.

Community-engaged performance tours aspire to reach the stage of empowerment on the aforementioned participation ladder by engendering an *I-You* relationship—a dialogue—between the academic institution, the community, and all participants. This occurs through a relationship involving reciprocal rights and obligations based on mutual trust and respect. This relationship progresses through two initial steps: narrowing the definition of community by identifying community partners who are interested in a partnership and willing and able to make meaningful contributions to the project and committing to a true democratic partnership characterized by an even balance of power, responsibilities, and privileges.[4] "Members of a community are active agents of change and they have the ability to find solutions to their problems, make decisions, implement actions, and evaluate their solutions" (Cole, 2006, p. 152). It is "about a shift in balance between the powerful and the powerless, between the dominant and the dependent" (p. 153).

Notes

1 "Classical" music is generally defined as music composed and performed following traditions associated with European musical principles and informed by Western culture.
2 Some institutions no longer use the term *stakeholder*, which can have negative connotations, especially for indigenous communities (Sharfstein, 2016).
3 It is worth noting that tourism is the world's most polluting industry. D'Eramo writes that the concept of *sustainable tourism* is inherently oxymoronic (p. 10).
4 There is no absolute definition of democracy; its usage is dependent on variables, including time, place, and circumstances. In the context of community partnerships, it can be defined as a relationship in which all members share common goals, responsibilities, privileges, and power.

References

AFCEA Tour Consultants. (2021). https://acfea.com/performing-arts-tours/custom-band-tours/
Boydell, T. (1976). *Experiential learning*. Manchester Monographs.
Buber, M. (1923). *Ich und Du*. Insel-Verlag.
Carlson, J., & Widaman, K. (1988). The effects of study abroad during college on attitudes toward other cultures. *International Journal of Intercultural Relations, 12*(1), 1–17. doi:10.1016/0147-1767(88)90003-X

Casella, R. P. (1997). *Popular education and pedagogy in everyday life: The nature of educational travel in the Americas* (Unpublished Ph.D. Dissertation). Syracuse University.

Caton, K., & Santos, C. A. (2009). Images of the other: Selling study abroad in a postcolonial world. *Journal of Travel Research, 48*(2), 191–204. doi:10.1177/0047287509332309

Classical Movements. (2021). www.classicalmovements.com/cultural-tours/

Cole, S. (2006). Cultural tourism, community participation, and empowerment. In M. Robinson & M. Smith (Eds.), *Cultural tourism in a changing world: Politics, participation and (Re)presentation* (pp. 139–161). Channel View.

Deardorff, D. K. (2020). (Re)learning to live together in 2020. *Journal of International Students, 10*(4), xv–xvii. doi:10.32674/jis.v10i4.3169

D'Eramo, M. (2017). *The world in a selfie: An inquiry into the tourist age*. Verso.

Dewey, J. (1938). *Experience and education*. Free Press.

Dierking, L. D. (2005). Lessons without limit: How free-choice learning is transforming science and technology education. *História Ciências Saúde-Manguinhos, 12*(suppl), 145–160. doi:10.1590/S0104-59702005000400008

Dwyer, M. M. (2004). More is better: The impact of study abroad program duration. *Frontiers: The Interdisciplinary Journal of Study Abroad, 10*(1), 151–164. doi:10.36366/frontiers.v10i1.139

Educational World Tours. (2021). www.eduworldtours.com/music

Falk, J. H., et al. (2012). Travel and learning: A neglected tourism research area. *Annals of Tourism Research, 39*(2), 908–927. doi:10.1016/j.annals.2011.11.016

Gibson, C., & Connell, J. (2005). *Music and tourism: On the road again*. Channel View.

Gilbert, N. (2005). Virtual roundtable: Advice from choir travel professionals. *The Choral Journal, 45*(7), 8–37.

Gmelch, G. (1997). Crossing cultures: Student travel and personal development. *International Journal of Intercultural Relations, 21*(4), 475–490. doi:10.1016/S0147-1767(97)00021-7

Helsel, B. R. (2015). To tour or not to tour: A case study in music education ensemble travel. *Excellence in Performing Arts Research, 2*. doi:10.21038/epar.2014.0105

Inhelder, B., & Piaget, J. (1958). *An essay on the construction of formal operational structures. The growth of logical thinking: From childhood to adolescence* (A. Parsons & S. Milgram, Trans.). Basic Books.

Janes, D. (2008). Beyond the tourist gaze? Cultural learning on an American "semester abroad" programme in London. *Journal of Research in International Education, 7*(1), 21–35. doi:10.1177/1475240907086886

Kolb, D. (1984). *Experiential learning: Experience as the source of learning and development*. Prentice Hall.

Laubscher, M. (1994). *Encounters with difference: Student perceptions of the role of out-of-class experiences in education abroad*. Praeger.

Laxson, J. D. (1991). How "we" see "them" tourism and native Americans. *Annals of Tourism Research, 18*(3), 365–391. doi:10.1016/0160-7383(91)90047-F

MacCannell, D. (1984). Reconstructed ethnicity tourism and cultural identity in third world communities. *Annals of Tourism Research, 11*(3), 375–391. https://doi.org/10.1016/0160-7383(84)90028-8

Mouton, W. (2002). Experiential learning in travel environments as a key factor in adult learning. *Delta Kappa Gamma Bulletin, 69*(1), 36–42.

Pearce, P., & Foster, F. (2007). A "universe of travel": Backpacker learning. *Tourism Management, 28*(5), 1285–1298. doi:10.1016/J.TOURMAN.2006.11.009

Pink, D. (2009). *Drive: The surprising truth about what motivates us*. Riverhead Books.

Pretty, J. N., & Vodouhê, S. D. (1995). The different interpretations of participation. *Focus, 16,* 4–5.

Ritchie, B. W., Carr, N., & Cooper, C. P. (2003). *Managing educational tourism*. Chanel View.

Robinson, M., & Smith, M. (2006). Politics, power and play: The shifting contexts of cultural tourism. In M. Robinson & M. Smith (Eds.), *Cultural tourism in a changing world: Politics, participation and (Re)presentation* (pp. 15–40). Channel View.

Scarinci, J., & Pearce, P. (2012). The perceived influence of travel experiences on learning generic skills. *Tourism Management, 33*(2), 380–386. doi:10.1016/j.tourman.2011.04.007

Sharfstein, J. M. (2016). Banishing "Stakeholders." *The Milbank Quarterly, 94*(3), 476–479.

Smith, V. L. (1978). *Tourism and behaviour*. California State University.

Stone, M. J., & Petrick, J. F. (2013). The educational benefits of travel experiences: A literature review. *Journal of Travel Research, 52*(6), 731–744. doi:10.1177/0047287513500588

Tosun, C. (2000). Limits to community participation in the tourism development process in developing countries. *Tourism Management, 21*(6), 613–633. doi:10.1016/S0261-5177(00)00009-1

UNESCO. (2010). *The 2009 UNESCO framework for cultural statistics (FCS)*. UNESCO Institute for Statistics.

UNESCO. (2013). *Intercultural competencies: Conceptual and operational framework*. UNESCO.

United Nations. Statistical Division, & World Tourism Organization. (2010). *International recommendations for tourism statistics 2008* (Ser. Studies in methods. series m, no. 83, rev. 1). United Nations.

Uriely, N. (2005). The tourist experience: Conceptual developments. *Annals of Tourism Research, 32*(1), 199–216. doi:10.1016/j.annals.2004.07.008

Werry, M. L. (2008). Shameful lessons: Pedagogy of/and/as tourism. *The Review of Education, Pedagogy and Cultural Studies, 30*(1), 14–42. doi:10.1080/10714410701566207

Wood, R. E. (1998). Touristic ethnicity: A brief itinerary. *Ethnic and Racial Studies, 21*(2), 218–241. doi:10.1080/014198798329991

World Tourism Organization. (2017). *About Cultural Tourism*. https://www.unwto.org/tourism-and-culture

3 Foundations of a Community-Engaged Performance Tour

Planning and Partnership

A community-engaged performance tour is grounded in a democratic, reciprocal community partnership. Without such a partnership, the ensemble will risk establishing an imbalanced relationship with the community, and the community might well view the ensemble as interlopers. Moreover, the community might well view the ensemble as interlopers. This chapter presents a typology and typical characteristics of successful community partnerships. Chapter 5 expands on this with information collected through hands-on experiences leading ensemble tours in Haiti and the Dominican Republic.

Campus Compact published characteristics of community partnerships in *Benchmarks for Campus Community Partnerships* (Torres, 2000, pp. 5–7). These are adapted and elaborated on in the following.

- **Genuine democratic partnerships** share a vision and have clearly articulated values. Such agreements are to be mutually beneficial and reciprocal.
- **Strong collaborative relationships** exist on trust and mutual respect. Partnerships value the bonds between people and acknowledge that networks of individual relationships build a community that deepens with time. They are organized and led through mutual respect and share responsibilities, risks, and rewards equally.
- **Sustainable partnerships become an** integral part of the mission and support systems of the partnering institutions. They are sustained by predetermined processes for revisiting the premises of the partnership, a structure that allows for evolution and growth, practices that support frequent communication, and joint problem-solving with a focus on both methods and outcomes. Partnerships are not immediate. They develop over time and are fluid, dynamic, and subject to internal and external changes.

Enos and Morton (2003, p. 25) build on these guidelines by proposing two types of partnerships: *transactional* partnerships, designed to complete a task with no additional plan or promise, and *transformative* partnerships, which explore a continuing relationship that will potentially transform both parties. Narrowly defined, a community-engaged performance tour tends to

DOI: 10.4324/9781003278696-4

be transactional. Two organizations enter a partnership with a clear purpose, goals, and outcomes. Time, resources, and personnel limit the project's scope, and each entity maintains its identity. In other words, after the project is over, they go their separate ways. However, like most campus–community partnerships, these tours have the potential to motivate participants to sustain their engagement and "create knowledge, transact power, mix personal and institutional interests, and make meaning" (p. 29). Thus, a community-engaged performance tour can form the foundation of a transformative partnership, where both entities focus on broader common goals and derive lasting meaning from related projects. They begin to view themselves as members of the *same* community, with common problems, interests, resources, and agency. In doing so, they transcend the common perception of campus–community partnerships, positing that the community has preexisting problems, and the institution brings resources, knowledge, and solutions (p. 29).

It is not necessary or productive to envisage a transformative partnership when contemplating a community-engaged performance tour. Institutional affiliations are as fluid and dynamic as any relationship. However, the idea of a lasting collaboration merits consideration. If both entities' leaders are open to the possibility, just one tour could evolve into an ongoing collaboration.

As an ensemble director, taking ownership of and thoughtfully evaluating all aspects of a campus–community relationship is crucial. Although this process is challenging and enormously time-consuming, it is the only path toward creating a collegial and reciprocal relationship with community partners. Successful tours and impactful experiences will occur only through hands-on, bespoke planning and development. Begin by working through the following foundational steps of initial tour development. These steps will determine the scope of the tour and provide clear guidelines to inform subsequent decisions.

- Develop a Philosophy and Mission
- Write a Mission Statement
- Select a Tour Location and Context
- Develop a Community Partnership
- Hire a Tour Company (or not)

Develop a Philosophy and Mission

An overarching philosophy will define and govern the tour and community partnership. Traditional performance tours primarily disseminate knowledge in the form of music, but a community-engaged performance tour is designed to share *and* discover knowledge. It is guided by the belief that members of the academy do not have sole possession of information and

Foundations of a Community-Engaged Performance Tour 37

competency and that the community is equally capable and knowledgeable. Recalling the *Benchmarks for Campus Community Partnerships* listed earlier, a community-engaged performance tour should aspire to accomplish three things: 1) enter into an equal and reciprocal democratic partnership, 2) develop a collaborative relationship based on trust and mutual respect, and 3) sustain the partnership over time.

Your tour should also support the mission of your institution. As one example, Cornell Wind Symphony tours intend to further the institutional mission to

> discover, preserve, and disseminate knowledge, to educate the next generation of global citizens, and to promote a culture of broad inquiry throughout and beyond the Cornell community.
>
> (Cornell University, n.d.)

A community-engaged tour strives to "discover and disseminate knowledge" and "promote a culture of broad inquiry" based on an expectation of an equal and reciprocal exchange of knowledge and information between the university and the community. Moreover, because the tour occurs off-campus and in the community, it has the potential to "educate the next generation of global citizens." However, this broad aspiration requires a more explicit definition of the kind of global citizenship the tour should foster.

Westheimer and Kahne's *What Kind of Citizen?* is frequently cited for classifying three types of citizens in a given community. According to the authors, *personally responsible citizens* act responsibly in their community and volunteer in times of crisis. The *participatory citizen* is an active member of community organizations and takes leadership positions within established social and civic systems and structures. The *justice-oriented citizen* evaluates and questions social, political, and economic structures, drawing attention to and trying to change systems that foster patterns of injustice (2004, p. 240).

The core philosophy of programs focused on personally responsible citizenship is to build moral character through volunteerism. The problem is that these programs risk reinforcing pre-existing stereotypes and biases. While students may "feel good" about their service experience, they may never consider the power and privilege dynamics that led to community challenges requiring the need for service.[1]

Programs aspiring to create participatory citizens encourage students to participate actively in existing systems in the community, for example, contributing to an established volunteer program. However, these programs typically do not prompt students to question underlying structures or systems that implicitly or explicitly foster inequality in the community (Westheimer & Kahne, p. 242). Moreover, through volunteerism, students may engage in an unequal relationship with the community, furthering the conditions they hope to alleviate.

Programs aiming to produce justice-oriented citizens differ from the previous two categories by deemphasizing volunteerism and examining all project members' power and privilege. While working with community members, students are encouraged to consider the established systems governing that community and the extent to which those systems have contributed to inequality. Programs of this type should be structured to create a balanced power dynamic between students and community members. Otherwise, the program may be self-defeating and may reinforce the power imbalances and cultural norms it sought to change.

Returning to my institution's mission statement, Cornell aims to use public service to "enhance the lives and livelihoods of students, the people of New York, and others worldwide" (Cornell University, n.d.). While I desired to support this goal, this statement requires some clarification. Service can easily turn into volunteerism, which can either implicitly or explicitly result in an unequal relationship between the "servers" and the "served." In light of this, as well as my privileged position as a white male on the faculty of an Ivy League institution, I opted to withhold service from my mission for the tours and emphasize the collaborative aspect of community-engaged performance, thus framing the tour around mutual assistance instead of unilateral service.

In addition to criteria such as those listed earlier, we must consider our students' backgrounds, maturity, and positions. My students at Cornell represent a diverse range of backgrounds and life experiences but, in many ways, are united in their relative privilege: most are between the ages of 18 and 22 years, enrolled in a highly selective university, single and without children, and at a point in life where their primary responsibility is their education. These realities led me to frame Wind Symphony tours around a social justice perspective. Students have the space to explore systems of power and privilege in global contexts, become more aware of their privileged position, and consider ways to serve the greater good through activism and engagement. They collaborate with community members on activities crafted with community leaders and aspire to achieve goals previously agreed upon by all interested parties.

It would be naïve to think that brief performance tours can solve social inequalities or bridge cultural divisions. That is not the point. Through pre-tour learning activities, guided reflection exercises, and the tour itself, students have the space to consider and discuss established systems that reinforce inequality based on social constructs, such as race and class.

Write a Mission Statement

Community-engaged performance tours compel students to take a stand concerning their level of engagement with the community. Will they be tourists *in* the community or partners *with* the community? Will they learn about the community in advance or travel without a relevant knowledge base? Will they commit to reciprocity and a sustained partnership or seek the passing excitement of an unfamiliar location? In my experience, students are informed primarily by their experience as tourists unless presented with a clear and logical statement of purpose and rationale.

Consider beginning with a concise mission statement. You can write it yourself or solicit students' input so they start understanding and investing in the experience. (This can be a good activity for an ensemble subset, such as a leadership group or a tour committee.) The mission can be revised before, during, or even after the tour; the key is that it remains relevant for everyone involved. Your institution's mission statement is a logical point of departure, especially if it includes goals around cultural competency. For example, Cornell Wind Symphony members contributed to the italicized portion of the ensemble mission statement.

> The Cornell Wind Symphony unites student musicians dedicated to the study and performance of emerging and traditional wind repertoire. *We explore music making as a vehicle for cross-cultural exchange and collaboration, and in doing so support Cornell's core values of public engagement, and global awareness.*

Select a Tour Location and Context

Ensemble directors often labor over the task of choosing concert repertoire. We endeavor to create musically and intellectually stimulating, technically appropriate experiences for our students. If we choose wisely, the students have a musically and intellectually stimulating experience and look forward to rehearsals. Each concert program forms a cohesive musical statement, and the concert season has a clearly defined progression that deepens and broadens students' musicianship. If we choose poorly, the rehearsal period can seem to last forever.

Community-engaged performance tours can be transformational for our students, but much like a rehearsal period and capstone concert, impactful experiences will occur only through hands-on, bespoke planning and development. The choice of a tour location must be based on your knowledge of your students, informed by your philosophy and mission statement, and in sync with your institution's mission.

Many tours, performance or otherwise, are designed to maximize the time participants function within their comfort zone—in an anxiety-neutral position. However, this is not an ideal setting for all learning outcomes. Daniel Pink (2009) wrote that humans tend to be unproductive when too comfortable (or uncomfortable) but are more productive when in a place of productive discomfort. In current parlance, this "sweet spot" of low-level stress—the position of productive discomfort—is optimal anxiety. Optimal anxiety is a worthy consideration when crafting a tour in which students are to be collaborators instead of tourists.

Crichton and Onguko (2013) coined the term *challenging context* to describe universal situations faced by low-income communities regardless of geography. Individuals in a challenging context lack access to many systems and conveniences taken for granted by more privileged communities. These include, but are not limited to, available and affordable electricity, clean water, adequate nutrition and healthcare, consistent Internet access, formal education, fair governance, and reliable police protection. It can be challenging to lead a performance tour to such destinations, which are often developing nations[2]; however, the tour can be immensely impactful for this very reason. If properly prepared and reflected upon, even a brief tour of a challenging context can inspire students to engage in, observe, process, and unpack situations that promote inquiry, critical thought, and changes to their position on issues related to power and privilege, dominance, and marginalization. The experience can stimulate critical evaluation of systems governing different cultures and how those systems shape individual lives and behaviors.

When considering a tour in 2017, I began by listing challenging contexts where my students would need to leave their physical and psychological comfort zones—locations where they would confront the realities of inequality, to which they likely had limited touristic experience, and about which they probably had limited information. I then selected a range of dates that would not interfere with my students' academic calendar or coursework: in my case, mid-January, which is typically near the end of Cornell's winter break.

Anticipating that traveling to a tropical climate in winter would be an added attraction for my students, I narrowed my search to relatively dry, tropical climates with a low likelihood of major weather disturbances.[3] These criteria led me to investigate Caribbean and Central and South America locations. Some of these—Haiti, in particular—are listed as at-risk locations by the U.S. Department of State. That does not necessarily preclude an ensemble from touring there although it does present additional challenges, as highlighted in Chapter 5.

Develop a Community Partnership

An attractive location is only half of the equation; plans are meaningless without the promise of a community partnership. What follows is an introductory guide for establishing such a partnership. My personal experience leading Cornell Wind Symphony tours and a review of current literature, primarily Barbara Jacoby's guide to partnership development, inform each step of the process. Additionally, many campuses now have a service-learning, outreach, or community engagement office that may have existing ties to communities you wish to visit and will likely be able to offer advice while making initial contacts and formulating strategies.

Identify Potential Partners

After selecting a tour context, identifying potential locations, and determining primary learning goals for your ensemble,[4] it is time to identify community organizations that might be a good fit for your project. Your campus outreach office may be able to help, but in my experience, the most promising leads will likely come from Internet sources and conversations with friends and colleagues. Much as you would interview a business partner, learn as much as you can about potential partners through their websites, social media presence, and news media. From these sources, assemble background information, including their history and current projects and initiatives. Do they appear to possess the assets and infrastructure necessary to help you reach your goals? Does their mission appear to be well-matched with yours? Do their current projects seem to be in line with those you have in mind? How might your institution's strengths and limitations complement theirs? Of course, this vetting process should be balanced with respectful consideration of the norms, standards, and cultural differences of the location.

Define the Scope of the Partnership

A community-engaged performance tour will not succeed without all participants' significant commitment. It is important to take this commitment seriously and determine your personal and institutional boundaries before contacting a potential partner. How much time and energy will you be willing to contribute to planning, administering, and leading the tour? Will it support your institution's mission or values? Do you anticipate being able to fund the tour through grants, institutional support, or private donations? With what level of risk will you be comfortable? Answer these questions honestly. If you are ready to proceed, turn your focus to your partner's expectations. It is helpful to think about the questions you might ask when planning an out-of-town trip to visit friends or extended relatives. What questions might they ask in advance of your arrival? Following are a few examples.

- When would you like to arrive?
- How long do you plan to stay?
- What will we be expected to provide: food, lodging, transportation?
- What will you bring with you?
- Would you like to come back? If so, when?
- How will you return our hospitality?

Now, answer the aforementioned questions as it relates to your prospective tour. *When would you like to arrive?* What will be most convenient for your students: winter break, spring break, or perhaps summer term? If you are not sure, speak with members of your ensemble. Today's undergraduate students often devote much of their summers to work or internships. Spring break is a second possibility, but students might feel homesick or burdened by rigorous academic schedules. Consider winter break as an option, preferably between two U.S. holidays: New Year's Day and Martin Luther King, Jr. Day. Traveling to a tropical climate in winter would likely be an added inducement for your students.

How long do you plan to stay? The duration of your tour will directly affect a number of factors, including the student learning experience, the project scope, and the financial cost. Consider the tour context, the amount of time you plan to spend in transit, the number of concerts you wish to present, and the estimated costs of essential services, such as flights and ground transportation. You must determine the most practical, financially viable, and educationally sound timeframe. If you plan to escort students to a challenging location, consider a stay of between seven and ten days. This length of time will enable students to acclimate to their surroundings, experience the place, and have meaningful interactions with their partners while mitigating the risk of becoming homesick or overwhelmed. Factor in at least one day in the beginning and one day at the end of the tour for travel and acclimation—without rehearsals or performances—and precede the tour with at least one day on campus for rehearsals and pre-tour learning activities.

What will we be expected to provide: food, lodging, transportation? Make a list of the most important resources you will need. Will you desire homestays, or will your students stay in hotels? Will you require ground transportation? Will you expect to borrow large percussion instruments or other equipment? Will your partners be responsible for providing for your safety and security? Arrange these items in order of importance, and prepare to discuss them honestly and openly.

What will you bring with you? Determine the approximate size of your ensemble and the complete tour party, including guests and/or chaperones—this needs to be only a "ballpark" figure. Make a list of items you plan to bring (e.g., folding music stands and all instruments except double basses) and others you would prefer to leave at home.

Would you like to come back? If so, when? Do you aspire to a transactional partnership of limited duration and scope, or a transformative partnership, which opens both organizations to a deeper level of collaboration and mutual understanding? There is no "right answer" to this question. Transactional partnerships may be perfectly acceptable to all participants, and they may not necessarily evolve into transformative alliances, which may be a satisfactory outcome for all involved (Jacoby, 2014, p. 75). Moreover, participants should feel free to change their opinion about the project based on their experiences. Institutional partnerships are similar to personal relationships: some grow deeper and richer over time, and others are better suited to limited timeframes.

Leaders must be transparent and honest about their intentions at the outset and as the partnership develops.

How will you return our hospitality? This question gets to the concept of reciprocity. It is of paramount importance to explain clearly that you desire a reciprocal relationship with your partners, as opposed to a one-off, touristic experience. Generate a list of options based on your campus resources and comfort level. For example, you may wish to host your partner's ensemble on campus. If so, consider the basic elements of how that might look. Might the project align with an existing grant opportunity? Will you be able to organize homestays or on-campus housing? More importantly, prepare to ask your partners for their "wish list." What are their goals, and how could you leverage your institutional resources to help them reach those goals? Resist any urge to force an agenda on your partners. Otherwise, you will risk building the partnership on an unstable foundation.

Start Early, and Take Time to Establish Personal Connections

You cannot take a "speed-dating" approach to partner identification, partnership development, or tour building—at least not if you expect to generate positive outcomes. After identifying a potential partner, contacting them through email and following up with a pre-arranged telephone call or videoconference is acceptable. If possible, avoid starting with a "cold call"; instead, ask a mutual colleague or a representative from your campus's outreach office to broker the initial conversation. After completing that step, remember that it is virtually impossible to cultivate a personal relationship through an intermediary, especially if the gap is substantial in terms of culture and language. Consider including a personal visit to the community as part of the planning process. Doing so will give you a better sense of the place; demonstrate respect, courtesy, and sincerity; and begin to assess partner compatibility.

Develop Common Goals and Evaluate Compatibility

As stated earlier, reciprocal campus–community partnerships require equal agency. Leaders of all entities must clearly understand their goals and objectives, and be willing to share them with their partners. Balancing this power dynamic is not always easy. Flushing out the details can sometimes be complicated, and community partners may not be able to identify their needs or desires or feel comfortable articulating them. Even if that is the case, resist the urge to dominate the conversation. Simply describe your goals, what you and your students can provide, and the student learning outcomes you hope to achieve. Remember that your ensemble is the visitor, and your hosts will possess much more information and resources in their community.

Stay in Touch

After completing the previous steps, schedule a conversation with your partner to determine how to proceed. Assuming that all parties agree, you must begin working on myriad details and logistics. This will require frequent, functional communication. Ask your partners how and when they prefer to be contacted, schedule regular video calls, and be prepared to keep the lines of communication open. Monitor your motivations by asking the following questions before and during initial partnership development initiatives.

- Is the partnership informed and governed by a shared vision?
- Is my partner contributing equally to our shared goals and decisions, or am I imposing myself and my institution on them?
- Are all members of the partnership sharing equally in work, risks, and rewards?
- Is the partnership reciprocal?
- How will the partnership be sustained?

The preceding steps are only the beginning of a fruitful, reciprocal partnership. Chapter 5 presents pertinent details from Cornell Wind Symphony tours of Haiti and the Dominican Republic, and Chapter 6 includes relevant logistical and organizational points.

Hire a Travel Company (or Not)

As mentioned earlier, a tour company can significantly simplify the touring process. The potential downside is that they also assume some level of ownership of the tour and, in effect, can lead conductors to outsource essential elements of their students' educational experience. If a community-engaged performance tour is the foundation of a reciprocal campus–community partnership, the agreement must be in an advanced state and well-understood by all interested parties *before* engaging a tour company. One must remember that tourism is an industry, and tour companies are businesses. Even if the company's educational goals align with yours, they will approach the project from a different perspective. Introducing a tour company into the relationship too early risks changing the project's scope, influencing its goals, and impacting unresolved decisions.

Alternatively, inform your potential partners that you are considering hiring a tour company, and give them your reasons for doing so. Perhaps, you are concerned about language or cultural barriers or are uncomfortable traveling to an at-risk location without additional support. Perhaps, you have found a high-quality company with expertise specific to the location you intend to visit or you wish to offload labor-intensive logistical work. These are all valid reasons for contracting a third-party provider. Your partners may be aware of

Foundations of a Community-Engaged Performance Tour

reputable companies with local representatives, or they may offer to help with logistical and travel support that a tour specialist would often assume. The key is that your partners are active and equal participants, even in the early stages of the planning process. If all parties agree, a tour company might even become a long-term member of the partnership. Chapter 5 addresses this point in greater detail.

Notes

1 Ivan Ilich's well-known 1968 essay *To Hell with Good Intentions*, which stemmed from a speech he gave to U.S. volunteers at the Conference on InterAmerican Student Projects in Cuernavaca, Mexico, reflects these dynamics by speaking to volunteerism's hierarchical implications, especially in international service projects.
2 The term *developing nations* collectively refers to Asian, Latin American, and former second world nations to distinguish them from the economically advanced "capitalist democratic" countries (Tosun, 2000, p. 618).
3 The Atlantic hurricane runs from June 1 to November 30, according to the National Hurricane Center (www.nhc.noaa.gov/climo/, 2022).
4 The pedagogy of community-engaged performance tours is discussed in Chapter 4.

References

Cornell University. (n.d.). *University Mission*. https://www.cornell.edu/about/mission.cfm

Crichton, S., & Onguko, B. (2013). Appropriate technologies for challenging contexts. In S. Marshall & W. Kinuthia (Eds.), *Educational design and technology in the knowledge society* (pp. 25–42). Information Age Publishing.

Enos, S., & Morton, K. (2003). Developing a theory and practice of campus-community partnerships. In B. Jacoby & Associates (Eds.), *Building partnerships for service learning* (pp. 20–41). Jossey-Bass.

Jacoby, B. (2014). *Service-learning essentials: Questions, answers, and lessons learned*. Jossey-Bass.

Pink, D. (2009). *Drive: The surprising truth about what motivates us*. Riverhead Books.

Torres, J. (Ed.). (2000). *Benchmarks for campus/community partnerships*. Campus Compact.

Tosun, C. (2000). Limits to community participation in the tourism development process in developing countries. *Tourism Management*, *21*(6), 613–633. doi:10.1016/S0261-5177(00)00009-1

Westheimer, J., & Kahne, J. (2004). What kind of citizen? The politics of educating for democracy. *American Educational Research Journal*, *41*(2), 237–269. doi:10.3102/00028312041002237

4 The Pedagogy of Community-Engaged Performance Tours

Pedagogy is the act of teaching, and the theory and practice of learning. As an academic discipline, pedagogy constitutes the study of transferring knowledge and skills to others in an educational context. Teachers' pedagogy shapes their actions, judgments, and other teaching strategies as synthesized by considering learning theories, learning goals, desired student outcomes, and student population. Both the theory and practice of pedagogy reflect different social, political, and cultural contexts; thus, pedagogy can be highly individual and foundational to a teacher's work. Two equally successful teachers in the same discipline may disagree on foundational pedagogical points. Indeed, a colleague once joked that pedagogy is "a four-letter word" because pedagogical discussions can be chronically contentious in faculty meetings.

In light of the ubiquity of performance tours in academic settings, there has been little research on related pedagogy. Educators lead ensemble tours of historically important locations, prestigious venues, and music festivals as examples of quality teaching, perhaps with the presumption that learning will occur organically. However, a clear philosophy and pedagogy paired with associated learning outcomes and rigorous tools to assess teaching and learning activities undoubtedly provide students with a richer experience.

This chapter presents a pedagogy for community-engaged performance tours supplemented with related concepts and activities. Community-engaged performance tours are learner-centered teaching activities grounded in constructivist learning theory. The tours emphasize curricular and extracurricular learning goals and create a learning culture that advances student outcomes in both areas.

Constructivist Learning Theory and Experiential Learning

Tours occur off-campus and usually in host communities. Outside the classroom, educators have the opportunity to craft unique experiences that challenge and stimulate all students equally, regardless of their backgrounds and positions. The following considerations apply to a wide range of ensembles

DOI: 10.4324/9781003278696-5

and student populations. While these have proven successful, educators must consider their unique student population when making pedagogical decisions and engage in hands-on tour planning and development. With that caveat in mind, readers will find detailed information pertaining to Cornell Wind Symphony tours in Chapter 5.

Most students grew up with a "banking" learning model: They prepare themselves to receive information and demonstrate the receipt of that information if called upon to do so, usually on a test or similar evaluative tool. Pedagogically, community-engaged performances align with Paulo Friere's theory of "problem-posing" education (1970), in which students become active participants in the educational experience and are encouraged to reflect and act on their experiences.

Based on the constructivist learning theory, Friere's approach has a long history rooted in the work of John Dewey and Jean Piaget, among others. While each of these theorists has a different perspective of constructivism, all posit that learners interpret their worlds actively and create their knowledge through various reflection processes (Fenwick, 2001, p. 10). Constructivism has two foundational principles: 1) knowledge is accumulated over time, built on a foundation of one's earlier learning, and 2) learning is essentially a social process. This theory is thus often cited by proponents of educational activities such as service-learning, which occur outside the classroom.

Many scholars embrace John Dewey's theory of experiential education as a theoretical foundation of service-learning (Jacoby, 2015, p. 6). Dewey asserted that people learn by doing and that education must be based upon experience to achieve the intended benefits for teachers and learners. However, Dewey maintained that experience is educative only if it satisfies two principles: *continuity* and *interaction*. In the first of these principles, the learner integrates aspects of a new experience and knowledge in ways that create new knowledge. In the second, the learner interacts with their environment and tests new lessons and hypotheses. Continuity and interaction form a foundation for learning (Dewey, 1938, pp. 35, 42, 79). Educators can facilitate this process by helping learners connect experiences in a coherent whole (Fenwick, 2001, p. 3).

Piaget (1966) wrote that people modify their views through attempts to resolve discrepancies between existing and new information. Thus, knowledge acquisition begins with experiences on which people reflect and incorporate into their preexisting beliefs and understandings. After observing children learning through play, Piaget theorized that the learning process includes two alternating processes: 1) *assimilation*, in which new information becomes a part of existing knowledge constructs, and 2) *accommodation*, in which newly acquired information serves to revise existing knowledge constructs or, less frequently, leads to the development of new constructs. In both processes, the learner participates actively and constructs knowledge based on their individual life experience.

In David Kolb's experiential learning theory (1984), people progress through a four-stage iterative cycle, in which experience transformation creates new knowledge.

- *Concrete experience:* A person encounters a new experience or situation.
- *Reflective observation:* The person observes and reflects on that experience.
- *Abstract conceptualization:* The person forms abstract concepts and conclusions based on their reflections.
- *Active experimentation:* The person tests their hypotheses in future situations, which results in new experiences.

While learners can enter the cycle at any point, the process generally centers around a specific activity or experience, making the theory a natural fit for community-engaged activities. Jacoby notes that service-learning "engages students in concrete experience followed by critical reflection on the service experience and, in curricular service-learning, with academic content" (2015, p. 6). The following adaptation of Kolb's model reflects the qualities common to community-engaged activities.

- *Concrete experience:* Students engage completely outside the comfortable and controlled environment of the classroom.
- *Reflective observation:* Students reflect on and attempt to understand and articulate feelings inspired by their experience.
- *Abstract conceptualization:* Students attempt to derive meaning from their experience and integrate that information with knowledge.
- *Active experimentation:* Students form hypotheses or strategies used and tested in the next phase of their experience.

A community-engaged performance tour is a concrete experience contextualized through curricular integration (i.e., music-making). The remaining steps in Kolb's model require reflection through which students process new information and assimilate it into their existing knowledge base. In a community-engaged performance tour, pre-tour reflection exercises are as crucial as rehearsals, and reflection activities during and after the tour are as educationally valuable as performances. Additionally, educators must guide and enhance students' reflections. From the outset of the tour through post-tour reflection, activities comprise four steps:

- engage students in a concrete experience as a starting point for building new knowledge;
- create conditions for educative dialogue during and after the experience;
- encourage students' focused reflection during and after the experience;
- provide support as students process potentially confusing, emotionally challenging, unfamiliar, and uncomfortable experiences (Fenwick, 2001, p. 18).

The preceding steps are discussed in detail later in this chapter. First, there is an important distinction between reflection and *critical* reflection. When people engage in critical reflection, they question their initial reaction to or judgment of a problem or event. Thus, critical reflection problematizes new knowledge that may otherwise become solidified as a person's knowledge construct. Eyler & Giles (1999, p. 202) writes, "part of the process of critical reflection is to confront uncomfortable observations and try to figure out why things are the way they are and why we interpret them the way we do." It is rare for genuinely transformational learning (e.g., a thorough and nuanced understanding of a problem or identification of possible solutions) to occur without critical reflection (p. 198).

Learner-Centered Teaching

In recent years, learner-centered teaching, also called student-centered learning, has gained significant currency in academia. This approach shifts focus from how information is delivered to "what the student is learning, how the student is learning, whether the student is retaining and applying the learning, and how current learning positions the student for future learning" (Weimer, 2002, p. xvi). Student-centered learning is informed by and related to many principles associated with constructivism and experiential learning. At the same time, educators must reinterpret their primary function from teacher to facilitator and endeavor to design and provide experiences that facilitate students' construction of knowledge.

Maryellen Weimer's *Learner-Centered Teaching* (2002) includes five areas where teacher-centeredness commonly appears in traditional classrooms: the balance of power, the function of content, the role of the teacher, the responsibility of learning, and the purpose and processes of evaluation. Learner-centered teaching constitutes a rebalancing of these factors.

- *The balance of power:* The instructor traditionally makes decisions about the course. In a democratized classroom, instructors and learners share a certain amount of power and authority over the teaching process. This construct can influence decisions regarding many issues ranging from content to evaluation and foster a participatory culture of learning.
- *The function of content:* Weimer asserts that teachers often focus almost solely on covering course content and creating a rigorous experience instead of creating realistic objectives and helping students achieve them. Consequently, learners resort to a "binge and purge" approach to memorizing information when confronted with excessive content. In such an environment, the successful student demonstrates the receipt of information, sometimes to the detriment of nuanced understanding and long-term retention. Weimer views content as a means of inculcating learning skills and habits, including study skills, time management, and self-expression.

- *The role of the teacher:* Students are accustomed to instructors making all decisions regarding content, conceptual interpretation, assignments, and evaluative methods. Weimer asserts that teachers should view students as seekers of knowledge who require guidance along their intellectual journey. If students are presumed to learn through experience, in-class activities should provide faculty with opportunities to help them clarify their understanding and assimilate the content in meaningful ways.
- *The responsibility for learning:* Weimer describes today's students as concerned primarily with earning good grades. If this does not occur, it can foster an adversarial student–teacher relationship and a competitive attitude among students. Student-centered teaching encourages students to take ownership of and responsibility for their learning by helping to design and shape the learning process. Such responsibility shifts their focus from grades to learning.
- *The purpose and process of evaluation:* Evaluation in a student-centered classroom should promote learning instead of merely assigning grades. For example, students can be taught to assess their work and that of their peers by asking critical questions and making constructive comments and judgments. Such a break from tradition does not happen naturally; the teacher must provide students opportunities to practice the theoretical and practical skills they are to perform. Strategies like these, Weimer asserts, will diminish test anxiety and draw a clear connection between learning and evaluation.

As described in the following pages, each preceding point applies to community-engaged performance tours.

The Balance of Power

Paulo Freire, mentioned earlier in this chapter, is credited as the founder of critical pedagogy, which Stage et al. (1998, p. 57) summarized as the use of education to

> challenge inequality and dominant myths rather than socialize students into the status quo. Learning is directed toward social change and transforming the world, and 'true' learning empowers students to challenge oppression in their lives.[1]

Community-engaged performance tours present educators with an ideal setting to help students wrestle with the status quo and examine structures and constructs that create inequality. However, this will occur only if a foundational climate is present in the classroom, where there is usually a status quo in the form of longstanding assumptions about power and authority. Tompkins (1990, p. 656) writes that it is not so much what teachers discuss in class but what they do.

"The classroom is a microcosm of the world; it is the chance we have to practice whatever ideals we cherish." Astin and Astin amplify that perspective:

> If those in higher education want students to acquire the democratic virtues of honesty, tolerance, empathy, generosity, teamwork, cooperation, service, and social responsibility, then they must model these same qualities not only in individual professional conduct but also in their curriculum, teaching techniques, and institutional policies.
>
> (2006)

In conventional rehearsals, the conductor assumes primary responsibility for correcting technical errors, molding the ensemble sound to their liking, and uniting the ensemble in their interpretation of the music. Stated another way, most rehearsals follow a "top-down" model. While rehearsal pedagogy is outside the scope of this book, there are ample resources for educators interested in experimenting with a more democratic, collaborative approach to preparing music for performance. However, such an approach directly affects the success of a community-engaged performance tour, which requires safe, inclusive, and democratic engagement. As such, the engagement begins by facing inward—among ensemble members and between the conductor and students—and ultimately faces outward—between the ensemble and community partners. A statement of inclusivity and relevant student expectations should be included in the course or tour syllabus, read to the students, and referred to when appropriate. The following statement is from the Cornell Wind Symphony syllabus.

> One of the strengths of this ensemble is that our members represent a rich variety of backgrounds and perspectives. All members are expected to contribute to an inclusive and respectful class environment by treating others with fairness, honesty, integrity, and respect. Civil discourse, reasoned thought, sustained and constructive engagement, and a collaborative spirit are required of all students in this course.

The preceding discussion of democratic engagement requires that the students have a robust discussion regarding the definition and concept of democracy. This preparation, combined with the tour, will enable them to deepen their understanding of both the basic tenets of democracy and the messy reality of putting such tenets into social practice.

The term democracy originates in the Greek *dēmos* ("common people") and *kratos*, meaning power or rule.[2] There is no absolute definition of democracy; its usage depends on variables, including time, place, and circumstances. Discussing democracy can be problematic as it risks politicizing the tour and potentially marginalizing students who hail from countries with nondemocratic governments. (It is worth noting that critical pedagogy has been the subject of criticism in education because it can be a means to politicize content and prioritize ideology over learning.) An apolitical definition of democracy is perhaps most appropriate for and well-suited to community-engaged performance tours and community partnerships. Following is one example.

> An even balance of power and agency characterizes a democratic partnership. All members share common goals, responsibilities, privileges, and power.

Students must also understand that democracy is an inherently performative concept; it relies on continuous engagement and input from all participants.

In summary, through community-engaged performance tours, students can critically examine relationships of power and privilege in their own settings and the communities with which they engage. With the instructor's assistance, they can reflect on this information and construct new knowledge, informing their actions and beliefs as individual global citizens.

The Function of Content

As stated in Chapter 2, a community-engaged learning tour can leverage music toward myriad learning outcomes associated with cultural competency, personal growth, and social skills. However, these outcomes should complement and not supersede musical goals.

Conductors in academic settings typically work with students for successive semesters, often over multiple years. However, most large ensembles traditionally offered in academe (e.g., bands, choirs, and orchestras) engage with only one primary repertoire: instrumental and vocal music in the Western (European) tradition. Moreover, mainstream music curricula in U.S. higher education typically focus on functional tonality, i.e., common practice music and related genres. Thus, one would expect that such traditions would form the basis of a performance tour program. However, this perspective can reinforce Western European music's hegemonic culture in academe, assert pedagogical authority as a form of power, and perpetuate the notion that institutions tour to disseminate knowledge instead of acquiring it—a notion that community-engaged performance tours strive explicitly to dispel.

Including one or two selections representing or honoring the host culture will not remedy the problem; such tokenism positions the host's music as an outlier of lesser importance or value. Instead, educators should devote a substantial part of the tour concert program to music from or related to the community and teach students about indigenous music from the community. Such an initiative requires study; engagement with, and advice from community partners; and perhaps the creation of new musical arrangements. It is, however, the only path toward an equal musical partnership. Moreover, it is the only way to guide students' understanding and appreciation of other cultures' music.

Additionally, community-engaged performance tours can enable conductors to broaden students' horizons in an organic, purposeful way by engaging with music from other cultures and delving into the question of *what music is* and how it interacts with culture. This represents a sociocultural approach to programming and teaching music within an ensemble performance tour context. In addition to exposing students to culturally diverse music, the tour goes further by

> creating inquiry-based spaces where learners are invited to discuss, question and interrogate the music experience from different social and cultural positions. Some contend that this approach to teaching provides students with a more realistic understanding of music and one more relevant to their lives.
>
> (Abril, 2009, p. 78)

Music-making is universal across all known human populations, but the term *music* has an English equivalent in only selected cultures. The English term partially borrows French and Latin etymons: French *musik, musique*; and Latin *mūsica*. Even if music were a globally recognized term, it could not be linked to a valid intercultural definition; it does not necessarily transfer from one culture to another and is open to varied definitions and interpretations. For example, the Arabic word for music (romanized: *musiqa*) does not map to the Western conception of the term. Qur'ānic recitation may sound musical to a layperson, but in the Islamic legal tradition, *musiqa* identifies specific non-religious aural arts (al Faruqi, 1985, p. 6). Most Native American languages and several African languages also have terms for individual types of music; however, they lack a comprehensive term for all music because a single noun is incapable of conveying the social elements, processes, and relationships of singing and drumming (Diamond, 2008).

Ethnomusicologists generally agree that music "is not a thing at all but an activity, something people do" (Wade, 2013, p. 7). By extension, terms ranging from *musician* to *musicality* are open to varied interpretations. Even musical quality is a matter of personal taste. For some, it is a purely aesthetic determination; for others, music's value rests with its expressive capacity (or the lack thereof). In light of these realities, a thoughtful examination of music may initially appear to serve only to highlight differences between people. Indeed, individuals commonly perceive their culture's music as more understandable, superior to, or having greater religious significance than the music of other cultures.

As one example, the history of Western music is rife with references to divine intervention and cultural hegemony. Popular belief credits Greek philosopher and mathematician Pythagoras with the divination of harmonic ratios (i.e., musical intervals) from the weights of a blacksmith's hammers. Although this myth has been proven specious, the Pythagorean and Platonic belief that the essential features of reality coincide with harmonic numerical relationships inspired music theorists to construct intervals and other pitch relationships from rational, mathematical principles. Ancient Greece is considered the birthplace of many elements of Western culture, and by the Middle Ages, scholars commonly held that the best of Greek culture passed by way of Rome into Western Europe. Through European colonization around the globe, this influence continued to spread up to the present.[3] In the 19th century, the term *classical* crossed over to music as a reverential term to earlier European composers, such as Bach, Beethoven, and Mozart.

Aside from culturally based preferences such as those listed earlier, music is equally powerful in illuminating cultural commonalities, as shown by the following examples of music production and consumption (Trehub et al., 2015).

- Music is cultural. Conventions and preferences with respect to structure, instrumentation, context, and meaning are all transmitted from one generation to another.
- Music is social. It can represent a mode of interaction. It is performed and often heard in group settings. Musical genres are often culturally stereotyped and linked to subcultures according to age, gender, and/or social constructs, such as race and economic status.
- Music is political. It is embedded within structures of power and influence. Where and when is a musical performance taking place? What music is being performed? By whom and for whom? Music can take on a political meaning, from solidarity to rebellion.
- Music is often used to express an identity. It can be emblematic of a group (e.g., a school song), a nationality, and an ethnic group (Wade, p. 18).
- Music is universally associated with emotion and ritual. Music is believed to affect our emotions: from pleasure to displeasure, to altered states of consciousness such as trance. Music is used to communicate with, honor, or serve deities. Music is often used in caregiving for its soothing properties.
- Music can easily be decontextualized and recontextualized by those who perform and listen to it. It can be assigned new functions or meanings (p. 19).

It is through these commonalities that educators have an opportunity to foster inclusivity and respect for other cultures in their student population and communicate that respect to their audiences. In the context of music studied and performed for community-engaged performance tours, the popular adage "you are what you eat" can be adapted: You are what you perform.

The Role of the Teacher

In a teacher-centered classroom, the teacher primarily distributes information. This method is in sync with a conventional "top-down" rehearsal model discussed earlier in this chapter. In a learner-centered classroom, the teacher delivers information and facilitates students' acquisition and retention of information. This approach stimulates students' curiosity and inquiry levels. It also motivates them to focus on a wide range of material, from general concepts to underlying meanings to successful applications.

Some students are naturally interested and academically inclined; others have greater difficulty focusing and tend toward surface-level understanding. For teachers, the key is to inspire all students to aspire to develop a nuanced understanding of the material. A prime method of doing so is to design academic activities that are meaningful and worthwhile. Biggs & Tang (1996, p. 37) write, "this is made very clear in problem-based learning, where real-life problems become the context in which students learn academic content." Such learning is a strength of community-engaged performance tours. Ensemble members tour not only share information but are also receptors of it. They not only perform for the community but partner with community members. Tour members visit the community and work with community partners to reach their institution's goals. The tour members are not mere tourists; they learn to examine critically broad and complex societal issues.

Crafting Learning Outcomes and Assessment Measures

Essential to a successful tour is crafting learning outcomes, teaching and learning activities, and assessment measures. The instructor should begin by drafting a brief statement of the course aims, such as the following example from a Cornell Wind Symphony syllabus.

> The aim of this community-engaged performance tour is that students will integrate performance of standard and emerging wind band literature and off-campus partnership with a community musical organization located in a challenging contest. In addition to normative curricular goals, students will develop and refine cultural competency and global awareness through associated learning activities and individual reflection. These concepts provide a basis for investigating systems of power and privilege in both local and global contexts.

This statement serves as the foundation for several intended learning outcomes (ILOs)—statements describing what a student is to learn or activities they should be able to perform after completing the experience. A set of five or six well-designed ILOs communicates an integrated and holistic overview of the course; additional ILOs risk diluting the course and establishing unattainable outcomes (p. 113). Each ILO should articulate: 1) the kind of knowledge to be learned (declarative or functional),[4] 2) the content or topic the knowledge is to address, 3) the level of understanding or performance achievement anticipated, and 4) any particular context in which the outcome verb is to be carried out (pp. 125–127).

ILOs use action verbs at the appropriate level of understanding or performance intended. Benjamin Bloom's well-known taxonomy of educational goals often provides a basis for developing ILOs. Initially published in 1956, a group of researchers and cognitive psychologists published a revision of Bloom's Taxonomy in 2001 under the title *A Taxonomy for Teaching, Learning, and Assessment*. The revision emphasizes using verbs rather than nouns to label each category, accentuating the cognitive processes by which learners accrue knowledge.

A foundational aspect of developing cultural competency and global awareness is acquiring knowledge, integrating that information with existing knowledge, and forming new hypotheses and judgments. Following are examples of related ILOs appropriate for a community-engaged performance tour of Port-au-Prince, Haiti, organized in categories of Bloom's Taxonomy.

Upon completion of the community-engaged performance tour, students will be able to:

- Remember
    - Describe substantive events in the Haitian Revolution and the founding of the Republic of Haiti.
    - Define *democracy* within the context of a campus–community partnership and list substantive benchmarks of a genuine democratic partnership.

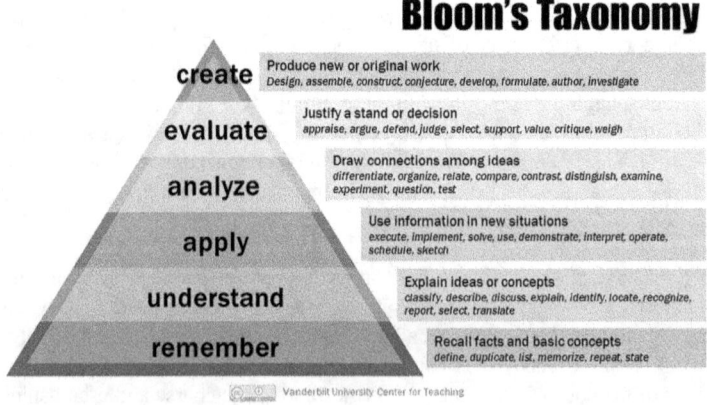

Figure 4.1 Bloom's Taxonomy (revised 2001)
Vanderbilt University Center for Teaching

- Understand
  - Summarize the geopolitical effects and lasting impact of the Haitian Revolution and the founding of the Republic of Haiti.
  - Explain the fundamental belief system of Haitian Vodou and list reasons for its racialization in the United States.
- Apply
  - Construct a theory of the relationship between Haiti's formative years as a nascent republic and the country's present-day struggles with political instability.
- Analyze
  - List and compare three leading sociopolitical roles of *rara* in Haiti.
- Evaluate
  - Cite and assess differences between Haitian and U.S. cultures and explain the reasons behind them.
- Create
  - Write a reflection statement including: 1) a meaningful observation or experience from the tour, 2) your initial reaction and any assumptions or judgments you made, and 3) how you refined your initial reaction by subsequent group discussion and individual reflection.

ILOs should be combined with *teaching and learning activities* (TLAs) to foster a holistic approach to learning outcomes. These include rehearsals, sectionals, performances, and social activities with community partners; individual listening, reading, and viewing assignments; small group discussions; travel journal entries; and guest speakers from the community.

Collaborative Learning

Education has done a good job of teaching students to be competitive but a far worse job of inculcating a cooperative, much less collaborative, spirit. For example, norm-referenced assessment (i.e., grading on a bell curve) pits students against each other because the highest earned score sets the curve at the top of the bell. This competitive culture is prevalent in the classroom and perhaps even in getting *into* the classroom. (Highly selective colleges are known to have low acceptance rates.) As a result of this stiff competition, students often learn to fend for themselves and prioritize individual achievement.

In contrast to courses in which students are responsible only for individual success, musical ensembles emphasize collaborative achievement. While students usually audition into an ensemble and are often seated according to their ability, the quality of the ensemble is dependent on every individual's level of performance. Regardless of their instrument, voice part, etc., all participants have equal responsibilities and share in the risks and rewards of performance. As discussed in Chapter 3, an equal relationship should also exist between college and community entities. Educators can draw a clear connection between the collaborative aesthetic of ensemble performance to a community-engaged performance tour.

The Purpose of Evaluation

Biggs (1996, p. 191) writes that "what and how students learn depends to a major extent on how they think they will be assessed. Assessment practices must send the right signals." Most collegiate educators do not require individual performance exams for ensemble members. From a pedagogical perspective, these exams emphasize individual achievement by connecting performance to a grade instead of the collective good of the ensemble. Moreover, students would be motivated to master only their part rather than learning how their part functions within the composition.

This practice should apply in grading community-engaged performance tours because many student outcomes are not musical. While a test would compel students to demonstrate an understanding of the information, it could risk devaluing the performative element of the experience. It is perhaps better to grade assessment tasks, such as those listed in the following.

- Written reflections
- Travel journal entries
- Blog posts
- Participation in group discussions
- Participation in engagement activities open to subsets of the ensemble (i.e., teaching or learning sessions with community peers)

For example, these tasks could form elements of a final portfolio to be submitted after the tour. For a community-engaged performance tour of Port-au-Prince, Haiti, the portfolio might include the following:

- A brief (400–500 words) travel journal entry written *before* the tour and based on one of the following topics: 1) something about which you are worried, concerned, or stressed; 2) an assumption or prediction about what will happen on tour; or 3) culture shock, broadly defined, and one related challenge anticipated.
- A brief (400–500 words) travel journal entry written *during* the tour and based on one of the following topics: 1) a group discussion prompt; 2) a personal observation, recollection, or "aha" moment; or 3) an artifact or photo collected on tour.

- A 1500-word statement based on personal observation or experience from the tour and evidenced by reflective engagement with one of the following topics:

  - Democracy, narrowly defined within the context of a campus–community partnership
  - The racialization of Haitian Vodou in the United States
  - Current social unrest and political instability in Haiti
  - The impact of deforestation on the Haitian climate and economy
  - Systems of oppression in a given society and the effects of those systems on citizens' lives and behaviors
  - Past and current U.S. government policies toward Haiti

One could argue that some of these assignments might prove challenging to grade objectively; however, not all knowledge, especially gained outside formal education, is quantifiable. To achieve higher-level learning objectives, students must be encouraged to share openly and honestly, take risks, posit original hypotheses, and form independent conclusions. The quality of the students' work and the depth of their understanding can be adversely affected if they believe that their primary goal is to demonstrate receipt of knowledge or make statements in line with previously stated tour objects.

Instead, they should be encouraged to take responsibility for their learning, embrace the opportunity to learn outside the carefully controlled classroom environment, and focus on the potentially messy process of developing functional knowledge. Just as an avocational learner might gain proficiency or even mastery of a skill or discipline, students may make transformative progress while engaging with the community despite having no formal training.

Designing and Guiding Student Reflection

As stated earlier, reflection is an integral part of experiential learning. Educators using an experiential learning model must prepare and equip students for reflection, lead them through associated activities, and support them as they confront potentially uncomfortable experiences, observations, or topics. Students participating in a community-engaged performance tour will need opportunities to clarify their understanding and assimilate the content in meaningful ways. A community-engaged performance tour happens primarily through structured reflection activities before, during, and after the tour; these create a safe space where students can control their learning and collaborate with their peers.

Conductors sometimes compare collaborative music-making to other group endeavors that are successful only if everyone participates equally. For example, a rehearsal for which only 25 percent of the members have learned their music is analogous to a picnic to which only 25 percent of the attendees have brought food: an unsatisfactory experience. The same rule applies to group reflection exercises; everyone must participate equally. From an educational perspective, reflection exercises are examples of social learning, where students learn from each other through discussion and cooperation. Such learning "is broadening, it gives opportunities for heightening self-awareness, and students like it" (Biggs, 1996, p. 69). There are many reasons for this; the primary among them is that participants develop a deep and nuanced understanding by comparing their interpretations and perspectives to their peers. They not only ask themselves what they believe but also why someone else believes something else (and which belief is better). Such activity can profoundly influence students to assimilate new and preexisting knowledge and form conclusions.

Students are generally unaccustomed to mandatory reflection exercises in a performance course, yet these exercises are essential in a community-engaged performance tour. In most cases, certain students are immediately comfortable sharing their thoughts and observations; others may make it through the entire tour without uttering a word. Rather than ignoring this imbalance, directors need to play an active role in prompting students with simple instructions, for example, "step-up" (into the conversation) or "step-back" (and allow someone else to speak). By asking students to remember those prompts during discussions and to respond if asked to "step-up" or "step-back," directors can ensure that there are no "bad vibes" in the room. Both instructions are meant only to facilitate high-functioning, equitable conversation. Instructors can ask particularly shy or reticent students to "step-up," and others can be encouraged to forego some opportunities to share.

The following series of steps helps to encourage and support learner reflection. However, this is merely a guide. Engaging an experienced practitioner to assist in designing and leading reflection activities is paramount.[5]

Promoting Honest and Open Communication

Students should feel that all honest comments, whether positive or critical, are integral parts of the reflection process. Instructors must foster an open and welcoming climate by: 1) acknowledging that the tour is to be intellectually and emotionally challenging, and it may stimulate feelings and observations that are difficult to understand; 2) encouraging open and honest communication; and 3) accepting and responding to potentially uncomfortable or upsetting feedback.

Teachers may appear to have all the answers, but it is potentially transformative for both teacher and student if the instructor is honest about their questions and concerns. A community-engaged performance tour requires everyone, from faculty to students, to leave their comfort zone. While appearing calm and in control of the situation, honesty is important.

Another potential impediment to honest communication is that students may feel compelled to comment positively about the experience. They might sense the need to demonstrate their attainment of the learning goals articulated in the syllabus. In light of current global conversations regarding equality and sustainability, they may feel pressured to be "enlightened" by the experience—to be suitably open-minded, empathetic, liberal, and globally conscious. Be wary of "rubber stamp" comments, where one student makes a comment (usually positive) and others simply rephrase it rather than striking out on their own. If that seems to be the case, consider problematizing this commonality and asking students to contribute something new to the discussion.

Peer pressure has the potential to exert influence and bias on group reflection. Unfortunately, this becomes increasingly likely as more students become invested in the experience. If they care deeply about the process and understand the amount of time, effort, and expense required to create the experience, they will be less apt to criticize it. If most students comment positively, others who feel differently may feel pressured to censor their opinions. For example, if most students claim to have been transformed by their experience and deeply moved by their work with community partners, an outlier might feel uncomfortable stating the opposite.

Setting Guidelines for Civil and Reasoned Communication

Students are sometimes reluctant to voice questions, concerns, or disagreements because they are unsure how to formulate an argument and/or express it civilly and respectfully, especially if the topic is controversial or emotionally charged. These require mitigation through clear ground rules concerning respectful and reasoned discourse.

Students should also be encouraged to formulate arguments using the following steps: 1) assertion, 2) reason, and 3) evidence. This process can be modeled by stating an unsubstantiated opinion (e.g., "Exams are pointless.") and refining it into a reasoned argument:

- The undergraduate learning experience would improve with fewer exams.
- The undergraduate learning experience would improve with fewer exams because frequent exams force students to focus entirely on short-term knowledge acquisition.
- The undergraduate learning experience would improve with fewer exams because frequent exams force students to focus entirely on short-term knowledge acquisition. By the semester's end, I'd forgotten the information I had learned for the midterm exam.

Explaining and Experimenting With Reflection Strategies

Before embarking on the tour, students benefit from basic familiarity with standard reflective processes. There are many models, but two are particularly useful in providing a structure for facilitating reflection.

One popular strategy derived from David Kolb's experiential learning theory is the *"What? So what? Now what?"* discussion model. It employs simple prompts to progress through three stages designed to help students process an experience. *"What? So what? Now what?"* is well-suited to informal meetings or "downtime" during the tour, such as bus rides or brief periods between rehearsals or before/after meals. Students can work on the second and third steps of the exercise in pairs or small groups, and outcomes from the discussion can serve as prompts for written assignments, such as journal entries and essays. *What?* The instructor or a group member describes an event from their experience.

- *So what?* Students try to unpack, interpret, and contextualize those events.
- *Now what?* Informed by the previous step, students develop strategies for dealing with similar experiences.

"Think, pair, share" is another popular collaborative learning strategy.

- *Think:* Students think (and potentially write) about their feelings or observations related to a clear instructor prompt.
- *Pair:* Students form pairs or small groups.
- *Share:* Students share their thoughts with their partner(s). After a brief sharing period, the instructor initiates a group discussion. Students may share their thoughts, or one spokesperson may share the group's commonalities or differences.

Regardless of the reflection model, fruitful discussions begin with simple, direct prompts and questions. The following examples could stimulate conversation regarding a specific experience.

- What was your first impression?
- Did your experience differ from your expectations? If so, in what way?
- How did you feel when you saw/experienced (a specific occurrence or situation)?
- What was the first thing you thought/felt?

Engaging in Frequent Discussions Throughout the Tour

Students participating in a community-engaged performance tour will likely experience myriad emotions. Some might be either psychologically or physically outside their comfort zone, homesick, stressed by the rigors of touring, or unsure how to perceive and process their experience. Check with them frequently and provide opportunities to share their thoughts and feelings. Reflection sessions may take various forms; employing multiple, contrasting methods is advisable to cater to different student preferences and communication styles. It helps to begin with an activity that encourages honest feedback in a fun, low-stakes setting. *Fist to five* is a tried-and-true ritual for assessing the "temperature" of the room and establishing a safe, participatory, and nonjudgmental climate (Hartman et al., 2018). To begin, a group leader selects an emotional, intellectual, or practical topic; defines a related question; and asks participants to respond nonverbally by holding up a fist or a selected number of fingers. The following is one such activity.

- Pose a question: "How overwhelmed do you feel right now?"
- Define the response: "Hold up five fingers if you're ready to tackle whatever the day throws at you. Hold up your fist if you're ready to crawl back under your bed covers and assume a fetal position. Or hold up any number of fingers in between." (Humor is helpful in setting the activity in motion.)
- Encourage participants to respond quickly and simultaneously.
- Ask everyone to look around and assess the group's temperature. Thank everyone for responding, and use their responses as a basis for a follow-up discussion or activity.

Fostering Individual Reflection

Through journaling, students can privately work through their thoughts and feelings before sharing them with others. This type of writing encompasses concrete observations, feelings, and thoughts to document and reflect on lived experiences. In contrast, a field notebook has a more externally focused documentary purpose and often includes drawings and collected samples (seeds, grasses, clippings, etc.). A *travel journal* is well-suited to brief tours because it is a hybrid form. It includes a documentary of encounters with another culture (noting both events and observations), recollections of interactions with peers and locals, and miscellany, including drawings, clippings, feelings, doubts, personal "aha" moments, and confessions.

Anchored in the belief that writing is thinking and that thinking changes, grows, and deepens through reflection, a travel journal kept before, during, and after the tour can augment learning. Before travel, writing and reflecting on one's expectations and fears, making predictions, stating assumptions, thinking in advance about how to manage stress and strong emotions, and setting personal learning goals can help one feel more prepared to arrive open-minded, curious, and ready for the encounter with another culture.

Organizing and stimulating the journaling process through prompts can help focus on the process, spur creativity, and deepen reflection and learning. Additionally, when the writing is shared, it can help educators determine where coaching or guided interventions might help.

Educators should be transparent regarding their expectations for journaling and encourage students to write freely and uncritically. Students require a reminder that, while rehearsals and performances are collaborative endeavors, journaling is for their own benefit. They should feel free to turn off their inner critic and allow themselves to make unexpected connections, have emotional reactions, and make concrete observations without filtering or refining their writing. With effort and a measure of diligence, journaling can become a regular habit and valuable resource for developing and reflecting upon perspectives and ideas. Appendix A of this book includes a list of journaling prompts.

Sharing Reflections Through an Online Tour Blog

Travel journal entries may also support group-learning and generate ideas for blogs or formal responses. Today's students are often comfortable sharing their thoughts through online platforms. Before the tour, consider asking one of your tech-savvy students to set up two reflection blogs: one for internal use and another for public consumption. The internal blog can be initiated before the tour and remain in place through the ensemble's return to stimulate student discussion and additional in-person reflection activities. With permission, students may copy posts to the public blog, keeping friends and family apprised of the ensemble's progress along with photos and videos. A blog post may begin with a question, prompt, photo, or description of an event. Students should be given a specific response deadline and perhaps instructed to respond only if they are part of an assigned subgroup (e.g., woodwinds and first violins).

Assigning Learning Partners

Biggs (1996, pp. 142–143) notes that grouping students in learning partnerships can provide a helpful and convenient context for discussion and mutual support. Especially on a community-engaged performance tour, students may need someone to talk to: to share concerns, seek clarification, discuss observations, check their interpretations, or simply confirm the schedule or timetable. The teacher should ideally match partners according to their mutual compatibility. Students then agree to collaborate as equals. They should sit next to each other in group reflection activities, consult out of class (occasionally during mandatory partner check-ins), and exchange telephone numbers and email addresses. Students should be encouraged to inform the teacher if a partnership is not working because of personal chemistry. In such cases, they should be re-partnered.

Engaging Students in Critical Reflection

An experienced practitioner should lead critical reflection sessions separate from other reflection activities. These discussions should occur soon after the tour has ended when students have returned to familiar surroundings but are still processing the experience. As with other reflection activities, one can begin with a prompt or recollect a particularly troubling or complex experience. The moderator should then evaluate how students' understanding of the situation has changed or developed. Then, additional questions and prompts can help students revise incorrect assumptions or reach thoughtful conclusions they may not have been able to process while on tour.

Summary

Community-engaged performance tours emphasize curricular and extracurricular learning goals and create a learning culture that advances student outcomes in both areas. This chapter has shown that tours can be learner-centered teaching activities grounded in constructivist learning theory. Tour planning must begin with a clear philosophy and pedagogy, and continue with the development of educational outcomes, teaching and learning activities, and assessment tools. Reflection is integral to such tours and must be emphasized before, during, and after the experience.

Notes

1 Friere taught Brazilian peasants to read, thereby empowering them to challenge corrupt political regimes and longstanding assumptions about power and authority.
2 While some communities in Ancient Greece were democracies, others were oligarchies. Athens practiced a direct democracy, in which all citizens had the right to participate in all political decisions and the exercise of power, and decisions were made by majority rule (although the term *citizen* was narrowly defined).
3 As discussed in Chapter 1, Athenian democracy and the Roman republic were foundational inspirations for the founders of the U.S., and Latin and Greek were the basis of the classical curriculum in higher education.
4 Declarative knowledge is knowledge about content (e.g., facts). In contrast, functional knowledge is knowledge about how to perform cognitive activities that involve the content, such as problem-solving and decision-making.
5 A representative from Cornell's Office of Engaged Initiatives participated in the 2017 and 2019 Wind Symphony tours of Haiti and the Dominican Republic. These will be discussed in Chapter 5.

References

Abril, C. R. (2009). Responding to culture in the instrumental music programme: A teacher's journey. *Music Education Research, 11*(1), 77–91. doi:10.1080/14613 800802699176

Al Faruqi, L. I. (1985). Music, musicians and Muslim law. *Asian Music, 17*(1), 3–36. doi:10.2307/833739

Anderson, L. W., & Krathwohl, D. R. (2001). *A taxonomy for learning, teaching, and assessing: a revision of Bloom's taxonomy of educational objectives* (Complete). Longman.

Astin, A. W., & Astin, H. S. (2006). *Leadership reconsidered: Engaging higher education in social change.* East Carolina University.

Biggs, J. B. (1996). Enhancing teaching through constructive alignment. *Higher Education, 32,* 347–364.

Biggs, J. B., & Tang, C. S. (2011). *Teaching for quality learning at university: What the student does* (4th ed.). McGraw-Hill/Society for Research into Higher Education/Open University Press.

Dewey, J. (1938). *Experience and education*. Collier Books.

Diamond, B. (2008). *Native American music in Eastern North America: Experiencing music, expressing culture*. Oxford University Press.

Eyler, J., & Giles, D. (1999). *Where's the learning in service learning?* Jossey-Bass.

Fenwick, T. J. (2001). *Experiential learning: A theoretical critique from five perspectives*. Information Series No. 385. ERIC Clearinghouse on Adult, Career, and Vocational Education. https://files.eric.ed.gov/fulltext/ED454418.pdf

Freire, P. (1970). *Pedagogy of the oppressed* (M. B. Tramos, Trans.). Seabury Press.

Hartman, E., Kiely, R., Friedrichs, J., & Boettcher, C. (2018). *Community-based global learning: The theory and practice of ethical engagement at home and abroad*. Stylus Publishing.

Jacoby, B. (2015). *Service-learning essentials: Questions, answers, and lessons learned* (1st ed.). Jossey-Bass.

Kolb, D. A. (1984). *Experiential learning*. Prentice-Hall.

Piaget, J. (1966). *The psychology of intelligence*. Littlefield, Adams, and Co.

Stage, F. K., Muller, P. A., Kinzie, J., & Simmons, A. (1998). *Creating learner centered classrooms: What does learning theory have to say?* ERIC Clearinghouse on Higher Education and the Association for the Study of Higher Education.

Tompkins, J. (1990). Pedagogy of the distressed. *College English, 52*(6), 653–660.

Trehub, S. E., Becker, J., & Morley, I. (2015). Cross-cultural perspectives on music and musicality. *Philosophical Transactions of the Royal Society B: Biological Sciences, 370*. doi:10.1098/rstb.2014.0096

Wade, B. C. (2013). *Thinking musically: Experiencing music, expressing culture* (3rd ed.). Oxford University Press.

Weimer, M. (2002). *Learner-centered teaching: Five key changes to practice*. Jossey-Bass.

5 Case Study
The Cornell Wind Symphony in Haiti and the Dominican Republic

The Cornell University Wind Symphony (CWS) is an auditioned ensemble that performs traditional and emerging wind band literature. The group typically includes 65 students ranging from first-years to doctoral candidates, and most of the students have majors other than music. The course meets twice weekly, for which students earn one academic credit. The previous chapters discussed the rationale for and the pedagogy of community-engaged performance tours. This chapter will outline fundamental steps associated with planning a tour and share anecdotes, challenges, lessons learned, and selected student reflections stemming from CWS tours of Haiti and the Dominican Republic.

Choosing a Location and Context

Before selecting a location and context, we must consider our students' backgrounds and positions, our goals and learning outcomes, and the mission and goals of our institution and school or department. As discussed in Chapter 3, I framed CWS tours around a social justice perspective to allow students to explore systems of power and privilege in global contexts and the reality of inequality based on race, culture, and geography. I hoped to help the students become more aware of their privileged position and consider ways to serve the greater good through activism and engagement. I did not expect that a brief tour would significantly correct social inequalities or bridge cultural divisions. Social justice pedagogies do not emphasize the creation of change; they create space to consider and discuss established systems that reinforce inequality based on social constructs, such as race and class (Westheimer & Kahne, 2004, p. 243).

Through public service, Cornell aims to "enhance the lives and livelihoods of students, the people of New York, and others worldwide" (Cornell University, n.d.). While I desired to support this goal, I initially opted to withhold service from my mission for the tours and emphasize the collaborative aspect of community-engaged performance. I believed such a characterization would better frame the tour for my students and, hopefully, stimulate discussions with our community partners around mutual assistance instead of volunteerism, which can either implicitly or explicitly result in an unequal relationship between the "servers" and the "served."

I began selecting a tour destination by compiling a short list of contexts, such as a universal situation faced by low-income communities regardless of division according to geography. I wished to offer students a destination that placed them in an environment outside their physical and psychological comfort zones and perhaps in a position of productive discomfort—in current parlance, optimal anxiety.

Although CWS tours are not eligible for departmental or college funds, we cobbled together funding through private donations, student fundraisers, and individual student contributions. Knowing that I would need to keep the costs within reason and assuming that airfare and lodging would be our most significant expenses, I focused on locations within a few hours of air travel. Anticipating that traveling to a tropical climate would be an added attraction for my students, I narrowed my search to relatively dry, tropical climates with a low likelihood of major weather disturbances. These criteria led me to investigate Caribbean and Central and South America locations. I began by selecting a range of dates that would support my geographical preference and would not interfere with students' academic calendar or coursework. With my students' input, I chose mid-January, which is typically near the end of Cornell's mid-semester winter break.

An attractive location is only half of the equation; the balance requires solidifying a community partnership plan. With this in mind, I initially focused on the Dominican Republic, partly because it satisfied my criteria and because I had a contact who taught at a reputable international school in Santo Domingo and had expressed an interest in collaborating. He felt confident that he could arrange homestays with his students' families and that his administrators would help us connect with underserved populations in the area. It was only through serendipity that I began to consider Haiti as a second tour location.

I learned through a colleague that The Rev. David César, a Haitian musician and Episcopal priest, and The Rev. Stephen Davenport had recently received Honorary Doctorates of Divinity from Yale University for their work with the Port-au-Prince-based Holy Trinity Music School (HTMS). César was the school's current director and conductor of the Philharmonic Orchestra. Based in the U.S., Davenport and his wife, The Rev. Tracy Bruce, were longtime supporters of HTMS and other Haitian organizations. Haiti was an intriguing location. I had never visited the country, lacked local contacts, and assumed that most of my students would be in a similar situation. Moreover, I presumed their impressions of Haitians likely rested on the predominantly negative reports from global news outlets. The catchphrase one often reads about Haiti is that it is the poorest country in the western hemisphere. Put more delicately, most Haitians live in a challenging context; they lack access to consistently available electricity, clean water, adequate nutrition and healthcare, consistent Internet access, formal education, fair governance, and reliable police protection—this was Haiti's most common narrative. In my subsequent research on the country's history and culture, I found a far more complex, engaging, and inspiring story than anticipated.

Learning About the Tour Location

Before planning a tour, one must gather essential information about the place and its people. Such information takes on greater importance when considering a domestic or international in a challenging context or subject to pervasive misunderstanding or racialization. Before leading a U.S. ensemble into a partnership with an entity in the Caribbean or Latin America, students must learn about the long history of U.S. interventions in the region. For example, in one six-year period, the U.S. invaded and occupied six countries: Nicaragua (1912), Mexico (1914), Haiti (1915), the Dominican Republic (1916), Cuba (1917), and Panama (1918). These occupations led to governmental and cultural destabilization that subsequently fostered brutal dictatorships, including Rafel Trujillo in the Dominican Republic (in power from 1930 to 1961) and François Duvalier (in power from 1957 to 1971), and Jean-Claude Duvalier (in power from 1971 to 1986) in Haiti.

Of all these countries, Haiti is perhaps the most misunderstood. One cannot fully understand contemporary Haitian culture without an awareness of the country's history. A brief synopsis of the information I shared with my students follows.

At the outset of the French Revolution in 1789, the French colony of Saint-Domingue was the richest in the Caribbean. French planters produced millions of pounds of cotton, about 40 percent of all sugar, and 60 percent of all coffee consumed in Europe. Soon after news of the French Revolution reached Saint-Domingue, the enslaved population, which outnumbered their oppressors by a roughly 10:1 ratio, organized a full-scale revolt in August 1791. Faced with mounting losses, France decreed the dissolution of slavery in 1794, but Napoleon Bonaparte still feared that the slave population had become too powerful. In 1801, Bonaparte sent the largest invasion fleet to cross the Atlantic—some 50,000 soldiers—to Saint-Domingue to return the colony to French control.

Meanwhile, U.S. President Thomas Jefferson, realizing the geopolitical importance of controlling the mouth of the Mississippi River, offered to purchase the city of New Orleans from France, but Bonaparte, believing he had the upper hand due to a secret treaty with Spain, declined. At the same time, France's efforts to reestablish control over Saint-Domingue suffered repeated setbacks. By 1802, France had become overextended and offered to sell French Louisiana to the U.S. This ceded control of the Mississippi River and the Louisiana territory to the United States, which eventually constituted 15 U.S. states. This ownership transfer made a significant amount of land for plantations and stimulated a sizeable increase in slavery in the U.S.

Back in Saint-Domingue, on January 1, 1804, the victorious leaders named the nascent republic Haiti after Ay-ti (land of mountains), the indigenous Taíno people's name for the island. The first Haitian constitution stated that only a Black person could be a citizen, but, in a unique non-racial interpretation of "blackness," anyone—white or Black—who rejected France, denounced slavery, and accepted that Black people ruled the nation was eligible for citizenship.

The Haitian Revolution and the subsequent founding of the world's first independent Black republic profoundly affected geopolitical history. Haiti's independence was a pivotal event in the battle over colonization of the Western hemisphere and African people's forced migration and enslavement. In 1807, Britain passed a law ending the international slave trade within its empire, and in subsequent years, France, Portugal, and Spain followed suit. This progress notwithstanding, geopolitical oppression of Haitians began immediately after the country's founding. U.S. and European powers ignored Haiti as a sovereign nation, and France demanded a payment of 150 million francs in exchange for diplomatic recognition. The U.S., Haiti's closest colonial neighbor, brutally occupied the country in the early 20th century and has continually meddled in its affairs. Desperate conditions and relative isolation plunged Haiti into severe debt, from which it has never recovered. The country has been disproportionately vulnerable to internal political struggles and economic and natural disasters.

When a magnitude 7.0 earthquake struck Haiti on January 12, 2010, the country was incapable of dealing with, much less recovering from, the deadliest natural event ever recorded in western hemisphere history. Estimates of the death toll range from 100,000 to 300,000 people. Some of my students were aware of the international aid response led by the U.S., which quickly raised 5.2 billion U.S. dollars. Global governments subsequently pledged roughly 10 billion U.S. dollars to help the country rebuild and recover; little of this funding materialized. The nation's infrastructure remains shattered. In late 2010, while still reeling from the earthquake, Haiti experienced the first modern widespread cholera epidemic, later traced to United Nations aid workers. An estimated 800,000 people contracted cholera, with a death toll of approximately 9,000. The massive global humanitarian effort had failed.

Only Haiti's most elite citizens have escaped the country's misfortunes, and there are clear distinctions between these elite and the rest of the population. Even a Haitian's relationship to language reinforces systemic inequality. The nation's constitution observes both Creole and French as official languages, but Creole is the only language spoken and understood by all Haitians.[1] Instruction in schools is provided in French even though some teachers lack fluency. Access to education is not universal in Haiti. Current practices sustain a legacy that stigmatizes Creole and reinforces its usage. Degraff (2010) describes Haiti as a country suffering from "linguistic apartheid."

Case Study 71

Learning About Potential Community Partners

One of the most crucial aspects of building a community-engaged tour is finding partners willing and able to engage in a lasting, reciprocal relationship. After gathering essential information about the locations, it was time to connect with potential partners so we could learn about each other and our respective institutions. Aside from my connection with a friend in Santo Domingo, I had no contacts on the island of Hispaniola or first-hand knowledge of Haiti. I began by exploring a relationship with Haiti's Port-au-Prince-based Holy Trinity Music School.

The Holy Trinity Music School (HTMS) is the oldest private music school in Haiti, and it serves over 1,500 students from primary grades to high school. Its story is particularly poignant. In November 2009, the school moved into a new building, which included practice rooms, rehearsal space, and a recital hall, the result of a decades-long fundraising campaign. Only three months later, the January 2010 earthquake ravaged Port-au-Prince and damaged the new building beyond repair. As of this writing, HTMS continues to operate in a temporary facility built in 2011.

I was unsure that members of institutions as disparate as Cornell and HTMS could join forces in a fully reciprocal partnership. However, an initial phone call with HTMS director The Rev. David César and The Rev. Stephen Davenport encouraged me to travel to Haiti and investigate the options. A few months later, I met the two at the Oloffson Hotel, a beautiful and whimsical oasis in the heart of Port-au-Prince. Our primary purposes were to get acquainted, articulate the goals that would inform our potential collaboration, and determine if the two organizations would be a good fit. During our meeting, Rev. César articulated two primary goals for a potential partnership: 1) to pool our resources and enable HTMS to reach a national audience, and 2) to draw both national and international attention to Haiti's rich history, vibrant musical community, and continued efforts to rebuild after the devastating 2010 earthquake. Although HTMS serves a large student population, the school can rarely travel outside the Port-au-Prince area due to a profound lack of financial and logistical support. We found common ground by crafting collaborative musical experiences around Rev. César's goals. Also discussed were possible venues throughout the country, primarily in the coastal cities of Cap-Haïtien and Jacmel, and listed numerous concerns about safety and security for both U.S. and Haitian students. Fortunately, HTMS is uniquely positioned to provide the infrastructure, staffing, and resources necessary for support and safety. The school is well-known and highly respected throughout Haiti and has a large base of support. Many alumni hold prominent positions in both government and the public sector.

Although I did not know it at the time, the Oloffson Hotel would factor heavily in my students' tours of Haiti and thus requires a brief description. The well-known hotel is in a walled compound, and its gorgeous architecture and lush vegetation serve as a buffer to the atmosphere outside its guarded entrance in the urban Carrefour Feuilles neighborhood. The Oloffson was one of the few hotels not destroyed in the 2010 earthquake and is a notable example of 19th-century Gingerbread architecture.[2] While strolling along the hotel's creaking floors and admiring the well-worn furnishings, one feels transported to an earlier era.

The hotel's proprietor, Richard Auguste Morse, is also the founder and leader of the *mizik rasin* (roots music) band RAM (Richard's initials). *Rasin* originated in the 1980s as a fusion of African-based Vodou rhythms and melodies with American rock and roll. RAM's instrumentation includes the core instruments of a rock and roll power trio—electric guitar, bass guitar, and drum kit—alongside *kòne* (long tin trumpets primarily associated with *rara*), *tanbou* (Vodou drums), and handheld Vodou percussion instruments such as the *fè* (a small metal instrument with a metal beater). Since the early 1990s, RAM has performed on Thursday evenings at the Oloffson Hotel; these performances have often been among the only social events in Port-au-Prince open to national and foreign individuals of various political allegiances and affiliations. I had the good fortune to see RAM perform and became determined to introduce my students to them and their music.

After spending three days in Port-au-Prince, I met with the Carol Morgan School (CMS) administrators in Santo Domingo. Establishing basic project goals and guidelines with CMS was much more straightforward than in Haiti because there were significantly fewer logistical challenges and safety concerns associated with traveling to Santo Domingo than to Port-au-Prince. While they share the island of Hispaniola, the two nations are worlds apart in many ways. Both suffer from endemic poverty, but the situation in Haiti is far worse. According to the World Bank, approximately 21 percent of Dominican citizens live in poverty, compared to 60 percent—more than 6 million people—in Haiti. The Dominican Republic benefits from a stable political system, robust governmental institutions, and civic programs. While tourism is currently not a viable industry in Haiti, it is the backbone of the Dominican Republic's economy.[3]

Building Community Partnerships and Designing a Partnership Agreement

While my initial visit to Haiti and the Dominican Republic was necessarily brief, it was an invaluable step toward building relationships and crafting the projects that served as the basis of the tour. On behalf of the Cornell Wind Symphony (CWS), I would build a partnership with the Holy Trinity Music School (HTMS). My partners and I would design my ensemble's tour of Haiti, and our students would rehearse, perform together, and help us achieve our respective goals. HTMS would host us, arrange for our safety and security, and help us earn funds from local and governmental sources.

Through a second partnership with RAM, I would present my students with the unique educational opportunity of learning about Vodou, *rara*, and *rasin* directly from musicians and practitioners. Together, we would spend five or six days in Haiti.

The Carol Morgan School (CMS) in Santo Domingo would provide an opportunity for me to reintegrate students into a familiar atmosphere before returning home. I believed that my students would be more apt to reflect on their experiences and share their thoughts and feelings after sleeping in air-conditioned homes and eating meals at chain restaurants or home-cooked by host families. In exchange, we would work with students in the CMS bands and perform two concerts, one for the public and another for a school assembly, during a two-day residency. This part of the tour requires further description. One of my primary goals was to escort my students to a challenging context. Such would not be the case at CMS, a beautiful facility housed on a gated 15-acre campus and similar in appearance and mission to U.S. preparatory schools. We would need to leave school grounds to engage with the community, which would necessitate another partnership—one I did not have the time or means to investigate. Were we to enter the community without a partnership agreement, my students would likely view themselves as volunteers, and the community might view us as interlopers. We would risk perpetuating the lopsided relationship of many community-engaged performance tours that I wished to avoid. As a result, I reframed the second portion of the tour as service.

School administrators and I drafted a plan that would benefit students from both institutions and the institutions themselves. Members of the CMS bands would benefit from: 1) sectionals led by members of the CWS, 2) side-by-side rehearsals and a performance with the CWS of Gustav Holst's *First Suite in E-flat*, and 3) attending a CWS concert. Members of the CWS would benefit from a seminar on Dominican percussion and a coached rehearsal of a wind band arrangement of the well-known song *La Bilirrubina*.[4] The CMW general student population would attend a CWS concert during a school assembly, and members of the CWS would give brief talks about their respective majors and career goals in selected CMS classes. Through the entire visit, we would honor Cornell's mission to enhance the lives of others through public service.

Partnership development depends on mutual trust, especially in early project planning. The primary partners must rely on each other to make preliminary decisions, communicate honestly and reliably, and generate interest in their respective institutions and student populations. During this project phase, it may be beneficial for all parties to enter into a written agreement, especially if the project is contingent on financial or in-kind support. While my partners and I generated substantial threads of related emails, I did not broach the subject of a formalized written agreement. This was partially due to my inexperience; each step of the process was entirely new for me. I hesitated to introduce another layer of complexity or potentially undermine the trust my partners and I was developing. In retrospect (and having reflected on a few sleepless nights), I would have done it differently: I would have asked my partners to join me in writing a document stating our goals, responsibilities, timelines, and financial obligations. As it was, multiple issues arose due to myriad unforeseen complications, from miscommunications to memory lapses. Fortunately, my partners and I could take it all in stride; however, given a different dynamic, these issues could have derailed the partnership.

The agreements described earlier and myriad logistical decisions took many months to resolve. In the months prior to the 2017 CWS tour of Haiti and the Dominican Republic, my partners and I shared countless phone and email communications. The Revs. David César and Stephen Davenport visited Cornell and spoke with my students. I made three separate visits to Haiti and one to the Dominican Republic. The Haitian portion of the tour presented numerous safety and security concerns, which my partners and I could only address through in-person meetings. César, Davenport, and I traveled and dined together, spent hours in traffic and roadblocks stemming from public protests, struggled to negotiate with local vendors, and visited potential concert venues. We devoted considerable time and energy to the project, but it could not have happened any other way.

The Revs. César, Davenport, and I crafted the following itinerary for the first six days of the tour. We tried to strike a delicate balance between keeping the students busy and fostering as much collaboration as possible without overstressing or exhausting them. In retrospect, the only thing that I would have changed was rehearsing on our travel day. It would have been better to schedule an ensemble meeting to reflect on our travels and prepare the students for the following day. The Port-au-Prince airport is chaotic for even one traveler, let alone a 50-person ensemble with instruments ranging in size from flutes to tubas. After collecting our bags, winding our way through labyrinthian parking areas to the buses provided by HTMS, and driving to our hotel, my students were exhausted. Additionally, I had grown accustomed to the city's heat, humidity, and chaotic atmosphere and underestimated how challenging these circumstances would be for some of my students.

Students began the tour from the Cornell campus in Ithaca, New York, USA. Campus housing was closed for the holiday break. Students in need of accommodations shared hotel rooms or stayed with friends who lived locally. It was more inexpensive to fly from New York City, even after traveling by coach and staying in an airport hotel.

Monday, January 9	1:00 p.m.	Rehearsal on campus
	5:00 p.m.	Coach service to JFK airport (dinner en route)
	10:00 p.m.	Check into hotel near JFK airport
Tuesday, January 10	11:50 a.m.	Fly to Port-au-Prince (direct)
	1:00 p.m.	Arrive, progress through customs, and bus to Hotel Oloffson

Case Study 75

	4:30 p.m.	Bus to the Holy Trinity Music School (HTMS) for rehearsal
	8:00 p.m.	Dinner at Hotel Oloffson
Wednesday, January 11	9:00 a.m.	Breakfast and free morning
	3:00 p.m.	Bus to HTMS for rehearsal
	6:00 p.m.	Dinner with HTMS students and faculty
	9:00 p.m.	Return to Hotel Oloffson
Thursday, January 12	8:00 a.m.	Breakfast
	10:00 a.m.	Ensemble discussion
	12:00 p.m.	Lunch
	2:00 p.m.	Rehearsal with HTMS at Kiosk Occide Jeanty
	4:00 p.m.	Performance at the 2010 Earthquake commemoration at Kiosk Occide Jeanty[5]
	6:00 p.m.	Dinner with HTMS students and faculty
	8:00 p.m.	Free evening at Hotel Oloffson with a performance by RAM
Friday, January 13	6:00 a.m.	Coach service to Milot and Cap-Haïtien, breakfast en route
	1:00 p.m.	Check into hotel and have lunch
	2:30 p.m.	Visit concert venue (Sans-Souci Palace)
	7:00 p.m.	Dinner and free evening at hotel
Saturday, January 14	8:00 a.m.	Breakfast at hotel, free morning
	9:00 a.m.	Optional visit to Citadelle Laferrière
	12:00 p.m.	Lunch at hotel
	3:00 p.m.	Rehearsal at Sans-Souci Palace
	7:00 p.m.	Performance with HTMS at Sans-Souci Palace

My contacts at the Carol Morgan School in Santo Domingo assisted me in booking a Dominican coach company to meet us in Cap-Haïtian and drive us to Santo Domingo. For additional safety, we hired two Haitian police officers to escort the coach to the border.

Sunday, January 15	8:00 a.m.	Breakfast at the hotel
	10:30 a.m.	Coach service to Santo Domingo
	4:30 p.m.	Arrive at Carol Morgan School (CMS) and meet host families
	6:00 p.m.	Dinner and free evening with hosts

Monday, January 16	8:00 a.m.	Breakfast at CMS
	9:30 a.m.	Sectionals with CMS junior high school band
	3:00 p.m.	Rehearse with CMS high school band
	5:00 p.m.	Dinner at CMS
	7:30 p.m.	Performance with CMS high school band
	9:30 p.m.	Evening with host families
Tuesday, January 17	8:00 a.m.	Breakfast with host families
	9:30 a.m.	Assembly performance for CMS junior and senior high schools
	12:00 p.m.	Coach service to airport (transportation provided by CMS)
	2:30 p.m.	Direct flight to JFK airport, then coach service to Ithaca (ca. 12:00 a.m. arrival)

Educating Students

It is crucial to educate students about a tour location's culture, history, and current events. Without an appropriate knowledge base, students will be less capable of processing their experiences and observations while on tour and may risk forming or reinforcing inaccurate assessments of their partners or the location. My students learned about Haitian and Dominican history, culture, language, and music through guest lectures, curated readings, and listening assignments. They had a weekly homework assignment, and I devoted approximately 45 minutes of our weekly rehearsals to lectures and discussions.[6] Formative assessment came through group discussions and peer-to-peer interaction, but I chose not to conduct a summative assessment. While a test or capstone project would have compelled students to demonstrate an understanding of the information I presented, I was reluctant to emphasize nonmusical outcomes with grades. In other words, I wanted to guarantee that students were not memorizing facts instead of learning their music, thus devaluing the performative element of the course.

The tour was not required for students in the course, although all were strongly encouraged to participate. Those who took part had the option to enroll in one additional academic credit; this provided compensation for the extra time spent on learning assignments and reflection activities and the tour itself. All students were required to participate in in-class learning activities, even if they had chosen to forego the tour. While a few students bristled at the notion of learning about countries they did not plan to visit, I included this expectation in my syllabus and emphasized it at the outset of the semester.

Ensemble directors are nearly united in one assertion: we rarely have enough rehearsal time. There are always musical adjustments needed and interpretations to unify. I often struggled to repurpose rehearsal time for lectures and discussions and recalibrate my musical expectations, but student feedback validated my choices. One of my students wrote the following after participating in the 2017 and 2019 tours.

Haitian history is the most beautiful, triumphant, frustrating, rage-inducing mess I have ever had the pleasure of learning about. In the lead-up to this trip, I was immediately drawn in by the historical resources that our director provided. It was fascinating, eye-opening, and terrifying all at once. While on tour, it took far too long for me to get out of my historicizing mindset and really engage with the present moment. But once I did, I started to understand more of the impact of our tours, both on ourselves and on our audiences (Meghna Srivastava, 2019).

In light of the time and effort it takes to undergo a tour of this scope, I have chosen to offer one biennially. Assuming a student participates in the ensemble for four years, they will have the opportunity to take two tours and, hopefully, develop a thorough understanding of the tour location.

Selecting Music and Programming Concerts

By design, community-engaged performance tours use music to help students from different locations and cultures to identify commonalities and collaborate as equals. Students at Cornell and our tour locations in Haiti and the Dominican Republic have a background in Western (European) music and can read a common notational language. My partners and I avoided a strictly Eurocentric approach to music-making by performing equal amounts of Haitian and American literature. In doing so, our organizations contributed equally to the musical product, and our respective musical cultures shared equal emphasis. Because the Carol Morgan School caters to an international student population, and our projects would focus primarily on reciprocal service, I prepared a traditional tour program around standard wind band literature.

An extensive search yielded few wind band compositions original to or inspired by Haiti. This compelled me to learn more about Haitian compositions, ask my partners for suggestions, create arrangements of existing music, and commission new works. For the 2017 and 2019 tours, I authored arrangements or transcriptions of nearly a dozen pieces of music, from *1804*, by elite Haitian composer, trumpeter, and pianist Occide Jeanty (1860–1936) to Charles Mingus's *Haitian Fight Song*. On behalf of the Cornell Wind Symphony, I also commissioned a new work from Haitian-American composer and former HTMS student Sydney Guillaume. Guillaume responded with *Renesans*, about which he later wrote:

> *Renesans* is my first work for wind ensemble. Knowing that the piece would premiere in my native country Haiti on the ninth anniversary of

the devastating earthquake of January 12, 2010, I wanted to write a work that was reflective and at the same time uplifting. Tragedies, misfortunes and loss often force us to re-examine everything, and they also give us an opportunity to start over, creating an exciting blank page for the future. . . . I imagine the strength and courage we gain after going through a dark time. The word *renesans* is Haitian Creole for "rebirth" which is something that we all go through in different ways throughout our lives.

(2019)

Drawing Connections Between Music and Culture

I selected compositions for transcription for musical and programmatic reasons and to stimulate my students' cultural and historical learning. The cultural racialization of Haitians stems from Haiti's U.S. occupation (1915–1934). Historian Laurent Dubois (2012, p. 211) noted that "the marines were white, and they brought "to the land of Black people" their own experiences and expectations from the racially segregated United States." Journalists followed U.S. troops into Haiti, and many contributed to sensationalized descriptions of Vodou practices. Beginning with William Seabrook's widely popular novel, *The Magic Island* (1929), readers were offered a glimpse at nighttime ceremonies of "sex-maddened saturnalia." The zombies that Seabrook claimed to encounter (and featured in the 1932 film *white Zombie*, flyers for which boasted "With these zombie eyes, he rendered her powerless; With this zombie grip, he made her perform his every desire!") led to cultural misunderstandings that irrevocably informed the global interpretation of Haitians. As Richard Morse noted, "the most popular Haitian word in the world is *zombie*. That is a reflection of the world more than it is of Haiti."

Any discussion of Haitian culture must include Vodou, which is in many ways "the soul of Haitian people" (Wall & Clerici, 2015). While the history of Vodou is in many ways tragic, it is far from mysterious. Thousands of Africans were shipped to Saint Domingue in the 17th and 18th centuries because European overlords had decimated the indigenous population. Africans were taken from different tribes and regions and required to abandon their beliefs and embrace Catholicism. To preserve their faith and overcome language barriers, they cleverly disguised their deities with Catholic names and portrayed them as Africanized saints.

A repeated observation is that Haiti is "70% Catholic, 30% Protestant, and 100% Vodou." Vodou functions as the country's ersatz health care system and features prominently in its politics, arts, and culture. However, Vodou is largely misunderstood in the U.S. and is most commonly associated with Hollywood depictions of sinister cemeteries, "spooky" occurrences, and needle-filled dolls. Through drumming, Vodou practitioners make themselves vulnerable so a *lwa* can enter the drummer's body. This "possession" is similar to being "filled with the Holy Spirit" in Christianity. A primary difference between Vodou and Christianity—and another reason for its racialization in the U.S.—is that Vodou ceremonies are primarily physical: participants move and dance. Additionally, strength and revolutionary spirit are associated with Vodou in Haiti. Scholars speculate that such characterizations explain historic Vodou fears in the Southern U.S. The concern was that if Vodou inspired a successful rebellion in Haiti, perhaps it could occur in other Caribbean nations or even the U.S.[7] I initially dismissed these misconceptions but had a bit of a reality shock when one of my students chose to forego our first tour of Haiti because her family feared a Vodou spirit might possess her.

The Vodou belief system centers around *lwa(s)* (spirits) that guide a person's life. Each spirit is an old soul with individual powers and perks to grant to its followers. As one example, Baron Cimetiére is one of the incarnations of Baron Samedi, the *lwa* responsible for guarding cemeteries and policing the intersection between life and death (*cimetiére* is French for cemetery). Cimetiére is usually pictured in a dark tailcoat and tall, dark hat, wearing dark glasses with one lens missing.[8] He carries a cane, smokes cigars, and is a notorious trickster. I used music as a tool to introduce students to Vodou *lwa(s)* and demystify the belief system. Donald Grantham's *Baron Cimetiére's Mambo* (Piquant Press, 2004) and his *Baron Samedi's Sarabande (and Softshoe)* (Piquant Press, 2005) provided such a connection. Grantham wrote that he "first came across Baron Cimetiére in Russell Bank's fascinating novel *Continental Drift*, which deals with the collision between American and Haitian culture . . . Voodoo is a strong element of that novel, and when my mambo began to take on a dark, mordant, sinister quality, I decided to link it to the Baron."[9]

More broadly, the aforementioned compositions contributed to my discussion of the intersection and synthesis of European and African Diaspora music through forced migration and enslavement during the French, Spanish, and Anglo-American colonial eras. The resulting creolized music and new genres irreversibly changed the global musical landscape. Stated another way, much of today's popular music is, to an extent, "world music."[10] Tracing the global journey of even the most straightforward rhythmic patterns makes this clear. For example, the *clave* originated in sub-Saharan African musical traditions and became the underlying tool for temporal organization in all African diaspora music in the western hemisphere, including multiple Haitian and African-American genres.

Figure 5.1 Clave pattern

Case Study

I programmed *Danzón No. 2* by Mexican composer Arturo Márquez (b. 1950) to describe the clave and other Afro-Caribbean musical materials. The reversed *clave* rhythm of two notes followed by three provides the foundational basis for *Danzón No. 2*. The *danzón* is, in part, a descendent of the French-Haitian *contredanse* (in creolized spelling, *kontredans*), which developed in Saint-Domingue. After Haiti gained its independence, both Haitians and French fled to eastern Cuba. This diaspora included the *affranchis*, perhaps more well-known by the Creole term *mulattos*, which resulted from race intermingling and who were privileged in Saint-Domingue society. For this privileged class, the *kontradans* served as entertainment and recreation. In the early 1880s, Cuba expelled thousands of refugees from the eastern part of the island. Many migrated north to New Orleans, which had a robust trade relationship with Havana. One can assume that the music and dance migration returned to western Cuba through this trade route. The *danzón* subsequently became the country's official musical genre and dance.

In addition to the foundational *clave*, the *danzón* relies heavily on a five-note musical figure called the *cinquillo* (also known as the *quintolet*), which figures prominently in much Afro-Caribbean traditional music, as well as sub-Saharan African bell patterns. The following figure illustrates the rhythm with conventional notation. Likely derived from Saint-Domingue, the *cinquillo* went on to play a prominent role in creole Caribbean music, especially contradance variants. In Haiti, it was used in the *méringue* (Creole: *mereng*; a whipped egg and sugar confection popular in 18th-century France), presumably because of the light and fluid nature of the dance or because of its clear, effervescent rhythms. Surfacing in Havana and Santiago *contradanzas* of the 1850s, it became the basic rhythm of the *danzón*.

Donald Grantham's *Mambo* completes a connection between U.S., Cuban, and Haitian music. The *mambo* began as a fast section near the end of the Cuban *danzón* and gradually separated from the latter dance form and gained individual recognition. It subsequently became well-known in the U.S., primarily through the performances of Cuban bandleader Dámaso Pérez Prado (1916–1989), who earned fame with hit songs such as *Mambo No. 5 (1949)*.

Most of the preceding information is specific to Haiti and may not directly apply to other tour locations. That notwithstanding, it is intended to guide conductors aspiring to draw curricular (i.e., musical) connections with the tour location and its culture. Without these connections, performance and cultural competency may remain mutually exclusive.

Figure 5.2 Cinquillo pattern

Touring in an Elevated Risk Location

The U.S. Department of State provides international safety and security information through the Bureau of Consular Affairs, which includes travel advisories, alerts, and country information pages. Every country is assigned an overall travel advisory level, from one through four, based on established risk indicators, such as terrorist activity, political violence, and criminal activity (2022). These are listed in the following.

- Level One—Exercise Normal Precautions: The lowest advisory level for safety and security risk.
- Level Two—Exercise Increased Caution: Be aware of heightened risks to safety and security. The Department of State provides additional advice for travelers in these areas in the Travel Advisory.
- Level Three—Reconsider Travel: Avoid travel due to serious risks to safety and security. The Department of State provides additional advice for travelers in these areas in the Travel Advisory.
- Level Four—Do Not Travel: This is the highest advisory level due to the greater likelihood of life-threatening risks. During an emergency, the U.S. government may be unable to assist. The Department of State advises that U.S. citizens not travel to the country or leave as soon as it is safe to do so. The Department of State provides additional advice for travelers in these areas in the Travel Advisory.

At the time of the first Wind Symphony tour in 2017, the U.S. State Department assigned a Level Two rating for Haiti, and before our second tour in 2019, the advisory was Level Three. These ratings gave me pause, as I was concerned about my students' safety. Nonetheless, my partners and I believed we could design a safe and positive experience for my students. First, we would not be traveling as individuals. Global Cornell, an international travel office, supports and facilitates safe travel for all members of the Cornell community. The office mandates that those intending to travel to an elevated risk location complete a petition requiring additional information and a rationale for the travel plans. All travel party members must submit their contact information to an international travel registry if granted permission. Should there be an emergency, the registration helps Cornell staff locate and contact groups and individuals to provide advice and resources. After my application was approved, a risk assessment specialist vetted nearly every element of the tour, from travel arrangements to the itinerary to an emergency shelter-in-place plan. The office also collected and vetted insurance documents from transportation and lodging providers.[11]

Second, my partners in Haiti provided honest, candid, and detailed information unavailable through my institutional sources. They advised traveling during early to mid-January, between the beginning of the calendar year and the Carnival season (Haitian Creole: *Kanaval*). During this period, Haitians typically observe an unwritten rule to suspend public protests and allow time for relaxation and Carnival preparations. This time is also during a season less likely to incur the most severe effects of Haiti's tropical climate; it is typically dry, and temperatures average between 70° and 80° Fahrenheit. There would be little risk of hurricane activity, and we would monitor local and international weather reports and change or cancel our plans if deemed appropriate. Moreover, my partners promised to provide support throughout our tour. They would meet us at the airport in Port-au-Prince, provide ground transportation in school-owned buses driven by members of their staff, arrange police escorts for our trips outside the city, and advise me on how and when to compensate the officers. (Law enforcement can be an entrepreneurial enterprise in Haiti.) Finally, I did not finalize my plans before traveling to Haiti twice individually. It was only through these experiences that I felt comfortable moving forward.

While safety and security were paramount concerns, it was important to strike a delicate balance between safety and luxury. My partners and I agreed that our students and staff should experience the same accommodations, meals, and modes of transportation. This would create a situation where all partnership members had equal privileges. However, this led us to confront additional problems: 1) our respective student populations had become accustomed to completely different levels of accommodation, 2) Cornell's legal counsel permitted the hiring of only providers and vendors that supplied specific insurance documents, and 3) HTMS was not in a financial position to match all of Cornell's required minimum standards. These factors made selecting accommodations a delicate process.

Selecting Accommodations

Locations in challenging contexts may not offer amenities common in most U.S. hotels. I found this to be the case in Haiti, where cities lack reliable electrical grids, and electrical service is often suspended during the day to protect the fragile infrastructure. Many hotels use gasoline-powered generators to power essential services, but some services are not fully functional until the grid is activated. Even in Port-au-Prince, nightfall leaves parts of the city eerily dark. People walk by the light of their cell phones and passing vehicles. Air conditioning, hot showers, and reliable Wi-Fi access often remain luxuries.

As a further complication, most Haitian hotels have a limited website presence. They frequently lack photos and reviews needed to make informed accommodation decisions. Based on my partners' recommendation, I targeted small hotels and negotiated from the position of booking the entire facility. While the hotel bars and restaurants would be open to the public, my students would be the only overnight guests, enhancing their security. After narrowing the search, my partners and I met in Haiti, interviewed the owners or proprietors, and discussed the safety and security measures required. To assuage my students' concerns and satisfy Cornell's legal and risk assessment specialists, I spent at least one night in every hotel, ate in every restaurant, and took photos of at least three guest rooms. I also confirmed that the hotels were in walled compounds with guarded entrances and offered essential amenities and services, including Internet access, secure rooms, and consistent access to filtered or bottled water.

In some cases, I needed to request safety upgrades that were unnecessary for their usual clientele and beyond the daily living conditions of many Haitian citizens. For example, if the rooms did not have glass or screened windows, I asked for screens or mosquito nets to be installed. The hotel proprietors were, without exception, welcoming and accommodating; however, for me, this was often an uncomfortable negotiation fraught with the possibility of offending my hosts.

My partners and I had an additional motivation to give my students an authentic experience. For example, in Port-au-Prince, we could have stayed at the luxurious Karibe Hotel, a gorgeous mountaintop resort with multiple pools, lush grounds, and a rooftop bar that would compare favorably to luxury properties in the U.S. My students would have undoubtedly had an enjoyable and relaxing stay, but they would have left Haiti with little exposure to Haitian neighborhoods and less understanding of the average Haitian's lived experience. Instead, we stayed at the Oloffson Hotel; as described earlier in this book, it is located in an urban neighborhood near the HTMS campus and offers a much more historically informed glimpse of Haitian culture.

My partners and I decided to present a concert in the northern coastal town of Milot. To reduce our expenses, my partners suggested that we stay at a church-owned campsite on the edge of town for two nights. Members from both organizations would sleep in cabins or tents; camp staff would cook buffet-style meals; and, without the usual distractions of cellphones and computers, we would organize activities to stimulate student interaction. Although this would likely have been a viable option, the campsite could not provide the required insurance documentation. Moreover, the students would have stayed in cabins or tents without locking doors and windows lacking screens or mosquito nets. My partner and I solved this problem by negotiating discounted rates with local hotels. Although the lodging was still cost-prohibitive for HTMS, we agreed that Cornell would absorb a greater share of the costs. In the end, our students enjoyed the same level of accommodation and, in some cases, stayed in the same hotels. While complicated and costly, the continued dialogue about these and other related issues led to a much more equal dynamic between our institutions and members.

Arranging Ground Transportation

In Haiti, I found ground transportation complex and challenging to schedule. Most areas within large cities are accessible by coach, but the situation deteriorates when traveling between cities, as the Wind Symphony did in 2017 (Port-au-Prince to Cap-Haïtien and Milot) and 2019 (Port-au-Prince to Jacmel). There is only one primary road between these cities, and any stoppage, whether due to an accident, everyday traffic, or a public protest, can add hours to the travel time. Roads are of uneven quality; pavement can suddenly yield to dirt or stone and then inexplicably back to pavement. Traveling in mountainous areas is difficult due to frequent flooding resulting from centuries of deforestation. A flight from Port-au-Prince to Cap-Haïtien takes approximately 30 minutes, but the 150-mile road trip takes an estimated 6 hours. (In January 2017, traveling by coach in heavy rain, the trip lasted nearly 10 hours.) Due to these factors, anticipated travel time can differ significantly from actual experience.

While planning a three-day excursion from Port-au-Prince to Cap-Haïtien, my partners suggested traveling in former school buses contracted through a local provider. While significantly less expensive than coaches, the company was not willing or able to provide the insurance documentation required by my university. HTMS could not afford coaches, which are significantly more costly, but my partners agreed to allow Cornell to absorb a larger portion of the cost (which we were, fortunately, able to do), and the two ensembles traveled together. This enabled our students to sit together and interact during the long drive. As with our lodging, this delicate negotiation threatened to undermine equality between our respective institutions.

Developing Cultural Competency

As discussed in Chapter 2, the term *cultural competency* refers to the acquisition of adequate knowledge about a particular culture, the holding of receptive attitudes about the culture, and the development of skills required to interact with members of the culture. Ensemble directors must develop and hone their cultural competencies before expecting our students to do the same. After two ensemble tours and seven individual visits to Haiti, I am still working to develop cultural competencies and manage a delicate balance between self-advocacy and cultural insensitivity.

As an outsider, I found Haiti to be a challenging place to conduct business, a perception confirmed by journalist Jonathan Katz after years of living in Haiti when he wrote that it is "a difficult place. No one, not even the rich, is insulated." Daily life in Haiti is "a trial by paper cuts" (2013, p. 51). Nonetheless, my visits were unquestionably worthwhile. Moreover, I have learned that planning a substantive project in Haiti will likely involve ambiguity. One must be willing to function in liminal spaces. To use a familiar phrase, this is simply "the cost of doing business" in Haiti, and I believe the significant rewards justified the risks.

Case Study   85

Working in Haiti has taught me to anticipate delays associated with "Haitian time," an approach to temporal organization that has little to do with conventional clock time. Events in Haiti are rarely punctual, but people seem content to operate with the relaxed assumption that everything will work out. Although I have not fully adjusted, I have developed a more nuanced understanding of the concept. Delays are to be expected because it is sometimes impossible to be punctual. Even under normal circumstances, one never knows when traffic could suddenly come to a standstill, a road could be closed, or a traffic signal has broken. As described in the introduction of this book, my students and I experienced a similar situation in January 2017 when we arrived 2 hours late to a concert. There was nothing we could have done; we simply did not anticipate the maddening traffic. However, it was still a mortifying experience; our Haitian partners were forced to wait for us and entertain the audience in our absence. It was only through their help, patience, and understanding that we were able to turn what might have been a negative experience into a positive one. My students learned that "Haitian time" is a way of dealing with the vicissitudes of life in Haiti without being overcome by them.

The concert described earlier was the capstone event of the 2017 CUWS-HTMS collaboration. The Revs. César and Davenport listed three goals for the concert: 1) to commemorate the seventh anniversary of the 2010 earthquake, 2) to highlight ongoing efforts to refurbish Sans-Souci Palace[12] and recast it as a tourist destination, and 3) to reach a new audience outside of Port-au-Prince. Together, we hoped to transform Sans-Souci Palace into a viable concert venue and present a gala concert featuring our respective ensembles. The project required enormous planning, fundraising, and infrastructure development. Majestic though it is, the palace is in ruins and does not have a performance space. We decided to build a wooden stage on its main staircase and a separate platform on the grounds for seated attendees. The entire area would be cordoned off to accommodate additional attendees and generate a secure perimeter. Security personnel needed to be hired. Portable lavatories were to be rented. While advertisements would be broadcast on television and radio and circulated through social media, special guests required notification through formal printed invitations.

I traveled to Haiti two weeks before the performance to check on the construction progress and was shocked to find that nothing had been built. Moreover, the funding promised by various Haitian organizations had yet to be delivered. I could not understand why time seemed to be standing still with so much riding on the performance. My partners and I arranged for meetings at various governmental offices, but they all seemed to follow a scripted progression. The participants exchanged lighthearted conversation in Creole and briefly discussed the matters in French. I understood neither language, and my only job seemed to be to wait politely. My partners reassured me that everything would be fine, but "Haitian time" notwithstanding, I did not share their confidence.

When I escorted 50 students to Port-au-Prince four days before the concert, the performance venue at Sans-Souci Palace remained untouched. Fortunately, construction began the following day, continued through intermittent rain, and concluded on the afternoon of our scheduled rehearsal. Lighting and sound equipment were under assembly when we arrived to rehearse. For the first time, I felt comfortable, breathing a sigh of relief.

This process evoked a range of emotions, from dejection to anger. Only after the tour did I realize why my partners had remained much more composed. I had expected the project to proceed on a timetable as in the U.S. I had not considered the complex history of relationships between Haitian and U.S. institutions, rife with stories of individuals and entities who arrived in Haiti with good intentions and grand plans but left before seeing projects through. My partners and their contacts had gone out on a limb to support the project, particularly those who were financial backers. With Haiti consistently in dire financial straits, any non-essential project would invite scrutiny. The backers could not move forward without a substantial demonstration of commitment, such as the arrival of my students. Even my visits were insufficient to assuage their concerns. It was only with my students' arrival that all involved parties had a guarantee that we intended to follow through with the performance.

It is worth noting that it may be challenging in Haiti and other developing nations to complete financial transactions as expected by a typical U.S. institution's business office. To an outsider accustomed to the immediacy of business transactions in the U.S., Haitian business dealings seemed mired in delays and byzantine complexity. Completing small, albeit essential transactions with cash is often necessary. I learned to keep a roll of U.S. dollars in small denominations on hand to compensate assistants, drivers, guides, and security officers. While these payments did not strictly follow my institution's guidelines, I had no choice but to adhere to local practices. I kept a written record and documented these payments as "gratuities."

Sustaining Partnerships: Planning for the Future

After the first Cornell Wind Symphony (CWS) tour of Haiti and the Dominican Republic in 2017, my colleagues and I crafted a plan to continue our partnerships. On behalf of the Holy Trinity Music School (HTMS), The Revs. César and Davenport joined me in committing to the following five-year plan. We aimed to foster reciprocity by holding an equal number of projects in Haiti and the U.S., including three CWS tours of Haiti (January 2017, 2019, and 2021) and two U.S. visits from members of HTMS (October 2017 and January 2020). In a separate conversation, Richard Morse (founder and leader of RAM) and I planned two RAM residencies at Cornell's Ithaca campus (September 2018 and October 2019) and RAM performances during CWS's subsequent tours of Haiti.

- January 2017: CWS and HTMS in Port-au-Prince and Cap-Haïtien.
- October 2017: HTMS Boys' Choir performs in Ithaca, New York, as part of a tour of the East Coast.
- September 2018: RAM holds three-day residency on the Cornell-Ithaca campus.
- December 2018: CWS director James Spinazzola guest conducts annual HTMS Christmas concert in Port-au-Prince.
- January 2019: CWS and HTMS perform in Port-au-Prince and Jacmel, Haiti.
- October 2019: RAM holds three-day residency on the Cornell-Ithaca campus.
- January 2020: CWS and HTMS perform at the Smithsonian Institution, Washington D.C., commemorating the tenth anniversary of the 2010 earthquake that struck Port-au-Prince.
- January 2021: CWS and HTMS perform in Cap-Haïtien in recognition of the tenth anniversary of the 2010 earthquake.

Unfortunately, due to political instability in Haiti and a lack of funding, the proposed January 2020 HTMS trip to the U.S. had to be canceled. The 2021 CWS tour of Haiti fell victim to the COVID-19 (coronavirus) pandemic. My partners and I navigated these challenges and designed new initiatives to sustain our partnerships through remote engagements. In December 2020, Richard Morse and members of RAM presented a four-part video lecture–performance series on Vodou, *rara*, and *rasin*. The series gave my students a deeper and more nuanced understanding of Haitian and Afro-Caribbean music. The Rev. David César and I planned to use web conferencing software applications to create virtual discussions, rehearsals, and applied instrument lessons with CWS and HTMS ensembles members. Unfortunately, HTMS had to cancel in-person gatherings due to the pandemic and the country's extreme political instability. We hoped to begin the project in the fall of 2021, but César's death in June of that year resulted in a suspension of the project.

Representatives of the Carol Morgan School (CMS) and I elected to repeat our 2017 residency in Santo Domingo in 2019. After concluding the tour of Haiti in Jacmel, we could travel back to Port-au-Prince, spend one night at the Oloffson Hotel, and charter a Haitian coach to take us across the border to Santo Domingo. (Due to increased political instability in Haiti, the Dominican coach provider refused to cross the border to pick us up.) We would then spend two days in Santo Domingo and follow the same general itinerary as in 2017.

Unfortunately, our entire 2019 tour suffered numerous canceled plans and altered schedules resulting from civil unrest and political instability in Haiti and the U.S. Some events were impossible to complete. Five days into the tour, we boarded a coach on a hot, sunny morning in Port-au-Prince and prepared to cross into the Dominican Republic. After nearly 3 hours en route to the border, we met with snarled traffic from a public protest. Large rocks, logs, metal chairs, and anything at hand blocked the road, and the air smelled of burning tires. Safety did not appear to be a concern. However, after hours of waiting for the road to be cleared, police instructed us to turn back. We returned to Port-au-Prince, spent another night in the hotel, and drove to a different border crossing the following morning. Given the political climate, this was not a trivial endeavor. We had to unpack the coach completely so guards could hand-check our luggage and instrument cases, first at the Haitian border and again at the Dominican checkpoint. An ostensibly straightforward process took hours to complete. Due to these delays, we missed our scheduled performance in Santo Domingo. Instead, we changed coaches in Santo Domingo and proceeded to the resort town of Punta Cana, where the students could relax and recuperate for two days before our return flight to New York.

HTMS is now under new leadership, and my partners and I face the challenge of maintaining our long-term partnership. While our personal relationships are strong, our respective student populations and administrations will soon have only distant memories of our previous in-person collaborations. When international travel again becomes safe and civil unrest in Haiti has subsided, we will have the opportunity to resume our five-year plan. After completing it, we will reassess the partnership and determine whether or not to continue.

Notes

1 Creole resulted from African slaves' efforts to speak the French that they heard when they arrived in the colony of Saint-Domingue. Creole would have been the most logical language after Haiti won its independence in 1804, but the elite, mainly white and mixed-race, population promoted the use of French.

2 This architectural movement integrates European influences with practical and aesthetic adaptations for the Caribbean climate. The term *gingerbread* was coined by mid-20th-century American tourists for its resemblance to the exterior trim of Victorian-era buildings in the U.S.

3 According to the World Tourism Organization, in 2019, Haiti logged 938,000 international arrivals, whereas in 2020 the Dominican Republic had 2.7 million arrivals, in spite of the global pandemic. As a point of reference, the U.S. had 45 million arrivals during the same time frame. (As of this writing, 2020 data is not available for Haiti.). (https://data.worldbank.org/indicator/ST.INT.ARVL?locations=HT).

4 *La Bilirrubina* was composed and recorded by Dominican singer-songwriter Juan Luis Guerra (b. 1957).

5 Kiosk Occide Jeanty is an amphitheater in the area of Champ de Mars in downtown Port-au-Prince. The facility was named after the famous composer, trumpeter, pianist, and conductor Occide Jeanty (1860–1936). The concert included performance by the Cornell Wind Symphony with members of the Yale Concert Band and the Holy Trinity Music School Philharmonic Orchestra and Choir. Haiti's de facto President Jocelerme Privert attended the performance and led the audience in a moment of silence at 4:53 p.m. when the earthquake began on January 12, 2010.

6 The ensemble rehearses twice weekly for a total of 3 hours 40 minutes.
7 The greater worry in the U.S. after the Haitian Revolution was about unrest, if not rebellion. This concern may have been legitimate; many Haitians were enslaved in the South before the Haitian Revolution. In that sense, Vodou was likely wrapped into a bundle of fearful concerns (Calvin, 2010).
8 The Haitian dictator François "Papa Doc" Duvalier (1907–1971) styled himself in the manner of Baron Samedi by wearing a Black suit and tie, Black bowler hat, and Black eyeglasses. This helped Duvalier hone his reputation as an all-powerful leader and earn favor with Vodou followers. It was successful, and Haitian lore was soon full of tales of Duvalier's dealings with the spirit world.
9 Practitioners and scholars typically use the spellings Vodou, Vodoun, or Vodun. Although still in popular use, the spelling Voodoo is generally avoided.
10 The term *world music* was used in academic circles beginning in the 1960s. It was adopted in the 1980s by record producers seeking to market newly popular African musicians and subsequently became a cover term for all non-Western music. (Denselow, 2004)
11 These documents proved difficult to obtain from Haitian vendors, none of whom offered comprehensive websites or clear contact information. Furthermore, tourism is not a strong industry in Haiti, and the vendors were generally not accustomed to providing their insurance information to international travelers. My Haitian partners solved the problem by visiting each vendor and taking photos of relevant documents.
12 Henri Cristoph, a leader in the Haitian revolution and self-proclaimed ruler of the Kingdom of Haiti, concluded constructions of Sans-Souci palace in 1813. An earthquake in 1842 left it largely in ruin. It is now designated a UNESCO World Heritage Site.

References

Calvin, M. J. (2010). *Toussaint Louverture and the American civil war: The promise and peril of a second Haitian revolution*. University of Pennsylvania Press.
Cornell University. (n.d.). *University mission*. www.cornell.edu/about/mission.cfm
DeGraff, M. (2010, June 16). Language barrier. *Boston Globe*. http://archive.boston.com/bostonglobe/editorial_opinion/oped/articles/2010/06/16/language_barrier_in_haiti/
Denselow, R. (2004, June 29). We created world music. *The Guardian*. www.theguardian.com/music/2004/jun/29/popandrock1
Dubois, L. (2012). *Haiti: The aftershocks of history*. Metropolitan Books/Henry Holt and Co.
Guillaume, S. (2019) Renesans. *Program note*. Portland, OR: Sydney Guillaume Music.
Katz, J. M. (2013). *The big truck that went by: How the world came to save Haiti and left behind a disaster*. St. Martin's Press.
Seabrook, W. (1929). *The magic island*. Harcourt, Brace and Company.
U.S. Bureau of Consular Affairs. (2022). *Safety and security messaging*. https://travel.state.gov/content/travel/en/international-travel/before-you-go/about-our-new-products.html
Wall, K., & Clerici, C. (2015, November 7). Vodou is elusive and endangered, but it remains the soul of Haitian people. *The Guardian*. www.theguardian.com/world/2015/nov/07/vodou-haiti-endangered-faith-soul-of-haitian-people
Westheimer, J., & Kahne, J. (2004). What kind of citizen? The politics of educating for democracy. *American Educational Research Journal, 41*(2), 237–269. doi:10.3102/00028312041002237
White Zombie. (1932). Directed by Victor Halpen. United Artists.

6 The Logistics of Leading a Community-Engaged Performance Tour

If you have come with me this far, perhaps you are ready to "take the band on the road." Whether in community, academic, or professional settings, ensemble directors often hold many unofficial job titles, including, but certainly not limited to, musical director, administrator, fundraiser, promotor, and finance manager. Organizing and leading a community-engaged performance tour will require skills from all these activities: planning, logistics, and organization. Depending on your chosen destination, it may be possible to outsource some of these tasks to a tour company. However, if you wish to travel to a location without a robust tourism industry, much of this work will fall to you to complete. The following steps must be addressed, preferably in order, in addition to the steps outlined in the previous chapters regarding partnership development and pedagogy. Additional logistical details from the Cornell Wind Symphony tours are available in Chapter 5.

- Secure Approval From Administration
- Craft an Itinerary
- Make Travel Arrangements and Select Accommodations
- Determine Individual Student Financial Contribution
- Include the Tour in the Course Syllabus
- Communicate With Students' Families
- Raise Funds and Awareness
- Prepare Students for Vaccinations and Travel Medications
- Make Arrangements for Students With Disabilities

Secure Approval From Administration

At this point in the process, you will have identified a tour location and laid the groundwork for a community partnership. You will have determined your mission and goals for the tour, its scope and duration, and your rationale for the chosen location and partnership. If possible, you have linked your mission to that of your institution and determined how the two align. Now it is time to request permission from the relevant administrator to commit to your community partners and move forward with more detailed planning. Toward that end, request a meeting to discuss your tour proposal. Organize your information in a clear, honest, concise presentation. Ask your partners to write a letter or record a video statement verifying their interest in the collaboration and describing how the project will help them reach their goals, or, even better, include them in a portion of your meeting via videoconferencing. Your overarching goal is to articulate the fundamental points: 1) the tour will support curricular and extracurricular learning goals, 2) the tour will constitute an equal and reciprocal campus–community partnership, and 3) the tour will be a safe and secure learning experience for the students.

Cornell's robust infrastructure supports international community engagement projects, including those in elevated-risk locations. Because I was not the pioneer in such a project, the approval process was relatively quick and straightforward. If that may not be the case at your institution, consider informally discussing your tour plan with several administrators, and try to find an advocate that can openly support you in the meeting. You may need to educate as well as inform. Be prepared to highlight the differences between traditional and community-engaged performance tours and to define foundational concepts such as service-learning and a reciprocal campus–community partnership.

Institutional liability is a primary issue that almost certainly will arise during the meeting. If you intend to travel to an at-risk country, speak in advance with a representative of your campus's legal staff or risk management office. Assuming that you can garner fundamental support for your tour, safety and security will remain paramount as you work with your community partners. Next, you will need to decide whether or not to visit the location personally and draft an itinerary.

Craft an Itinerary

With your community partners, craft an itinerary that will foster a balance between music-making and cultural exposure, action with relaxation, and experience with time for reflection. Minor details can be added and changed throughout the lead-up to the tour. First, set the duration of the tour, locations you wish to visit, concert venues and tentative dates, travel arrangements, and accommodations. Include time for on-campus pre-tour rehearsals and meetings. A colleague once told me that a tour should *crescendo* to the end, meaning that the most exciting and energizing events and performances should occur near the tour's conclusion. Try to relax the daily schedule gradually and allow students more downtime as the tour progresses. The students should arrive home tired and happy, not exhausted and harried.

Make Travel Arrangements and Select Accommodations

Flight arrangements are not specific to a community-engaged tour. Consider working with your institution's preferred travel agency to find the best possible fares and schedules, and then consult your partners to identify the options that will be the best fit for your project. Travel arrangements are likely included in the tour package if you have chosen to work with a tour provider.

Choosing accommodations can be significantly more complicated, especially if you choose a challenging context similar to Haiti. While students must be safe, secure, and comfortable, they should remain engaged with the community. Look for hotels that are secure but modest—where participants will feel safe and able to relax in an unfamiliar environment. Ask your community partners for recommendations and references, and learn as much as possible from Internet sources, such as hotel websites and travel blogs. Chains such as Hilton and IBIS can simplify the search by guaranteeing an expected standard, but privately owned hotels will likely be cheaper and more interesting (as was my experience in Port-au-Prince). If possible, all members of the tour group should stay in the same hotel to facilitate a fast response in case of an emergency.

If you plan a tour to an at-risk location, there is no substitute for visiting the prospective sites individually. Speak with the owners or proprietors, tour the facility, stay in a guest room, and document your visit with photos. A site visit is an ideal opportunity to discuss safety and security concerns and to negotiate particulars such as room rates, meals, and food allergies. Be sure to request an interpreter if you do not speak the local language. Following is a partial list of important safety and security features.

- Secure building or property perimeter
- Uninterrupted front desk or lobby monitoring
- Armed guard if appropriate
- Well-lit grounds and hallways
- Security cameras
- Clear emergency exit signage
- Smoke alarms in every room
- Lockable doors and windows
- Safe drinking water on premises
- Mosquito netting where applicable

Develop a Budget and Student Financial Commitment

After establishing the approximate costs of lodging, meals, and transportation, you will likely have sufficient information to estimate the entire cost of the tour, divide that figure by the number of participating students, and, if applicable, generate an individual student financial contribution. If you have hired a tour company, their quote will likely provide you with only one figure: the total cost for each student. For Cornell Wind Symphony tours of Haiti and the Dominican Republic, I based the student commitment on the cost of travel from New York to Port-au-Prince, which included coach service from Ithaca to New York City, and a direct, round-trip flight to Port-au-Prince. The flight was $525, and the $2,700 coach fee would be distributed equally between all members. Approximately 60 students typically comprise the Cornell Wind Symphony. Based on my calculations, 46 students needed to participate in the trip to be musically viable (i.e., to guarantee full instrumentation). Using that number, an individual base contribution of $584 covered each student's flight and domestic coach service. I then added the quotes for accommodations and ground transportation in tour locations (approximately $35,000), divided by 46 students, and arrived at a student contribution of $800. After discussing this figure with students and colleagues, I found it to be a financial "sweet spot" for my student population: more might be cost-prohibitive for some students, and less would place an undue burden on the ensemble.

A plan for students requiring financial assistance is required. I chose to reserve additional funds to assist students who would otherwise forego the tour for financial reasons. Fortunately, Cornell offered students the opportunity to apply for a travel grant through the Off-Campus Opportunity Fund, which is predominantly for short-term programs when financial aid is less available. Ensemble fundraising was used to support individual students with additional financial concerns.

Include the Tour in the Course Syllabus

Your syllabus should include the following elements:

- Definition of and rationale for community-engaged performance tours
- Participation requirements and individual financial contribution
- Explanation of student expectations and responsibilities
- Grading implications
- Tentative itinerary

Regardless of the discipline or student population, teaching involves some salesmanship. It is not enough merely to explain the material; it must be made interesting, understandable, and accessible. In this step, you begin to "sell" the tour to your students by: 1) outlining your expectations for them and 2) explaining how the tour will benefit them and enrich their ensemble experience. Begin by defining community-engaged performance tours and explaining how they differ from traditional tours. Next, list your goals for the tour, and describe how they support the mission of your department, school, and college or university. If possible, include a brief statement of support from an administrator, or invite the relevant person to speak to the students. Next, outline student expectations, deadlines, and projected financial contributions.

This step focuses on using language to tell the story of your community engagement project. The document you will write, along with all of your verbal and written communications, should foster a psychologically safe, inclusive, and respectful environment, and establish the tone of your community partnership. Before beginning, it may be helpful to review preferred terms for non-stigmatizing, bias-free language.[1] The following statements are from the Cornell Wind Symphony syllabus.

Overview

In addition to making music, the Cornell Wind Symphony is devoted to the exploration of music as a vehicle for cultural exchange, service, global awareness, and social change. Toward that end, in January we will embark on a ten-day community-engaged performance tour of Haiti and the Dominican Republic. The tour will not be a singular experience, but rather the logical conclusion of the fall semester (much as our concerts are the logical conclusions of the rehearsal process). Beginning with the first rehearsal, we will prepare ourselves by performing relevant music, learning about our host countries, discussing community engagement, and exploring the myriad ways in which our ensemble can become more powerful than the sum of our individual identities.

You will be asked to participate in brief individual and group reflection activities before, during, and after the tour. To be clear, these activities will not be optional. Assignments to be turned in (e.g., journal entries and reflection statements) will not be graded, but rather marked for completion and factored into your class participation grade.

Participation in the tour is not mandatory but strongly encouraged. Whether or not you choose to participate, you will be responsible for all pre-tour activities and assignments. All participants may choose to register for one additional academic credit.[2]

Most of our expenses will be supported by private donations, but all members who participate in the tour will also be asked to make the following financial contribution.

- Flight: $584.00
- Travel agency booking fee: $15
- Shared ensemble fees: $216
- TOTAL: $800

The following are your payment deadlines.

- Tuesday, October 15, 6:30pm: Tour commitment letter and $50 non-refundable deposit
- Tuesday, December 1, 6:30pm: Remaining balance due

The Logistics of Leading a Community-Engaged Performance Tour 95

Financial Assistance

The CU Wind Symphony believes no student should forego the tour for financial reasons. Students requiring financial assistance will have the opportunity to apply for a travel grant through the Off-Campus Opportunity Fund (OCOF). OCOF is predominantly for short-term programs when financial aid is less available. Students experiencing greater financial concerns should speak with the instructor. The ensemble will make every effort to help, and all conversations will be held in strict confidence.

Letter of Commitment & Deposit

In two weeks, you will be asked to sign a commitment letter. This tour will be possible only if the majority of our ensemble chooses to participate. Please speak with your parents about it immediately, and encourage them to contact me with any questions or concerns. You will also be responsible for a $50 nonrefundable deposit, which will be passed on to the airline to secure our advance booking.

Following is a copy of the letter you will be asked to sign. While legally nonbinding, I am counting on you to thoughtfully consider the opportunity and hold yourself to your commitment.

I am planning to participate in the Wind Symphony tour of Haiti and the Dominican Republic as described in class and in the course syllabus. I understand that I am expected to be on campus at 10am on January 7th for a pre-tour rehearsal.

I understand that I will be responsible for a tour payment not to exceed $750. The first $50 is nonrefundable, and must be paid no later than 6:30pm on October 15. The remainder is due on Tuesday, December 1.

Itinerary

Throughout the summer, I worked with colleagues and community partners to draft the following itinerary. All aspects of the tour have been evaluated from a risk-management standpoint with an overarching goal of providing you with an entirely positive experience. I have personally traveled the entire route, stayed in every hotel, and eaten at every restaurant. The itinerary is subject to minor changes.

(Readers will find the CWS 2017 tour itinerary in Chapter 5)

Communicate With Students' Families

The importance of this step will depend upon institutional guidelines and the age range of your student population. While it is not a requirement for collegiate educators to inform students' parents of curricular initiatives, I felt it was important when considering travel to an at-risk location to share information, invite questions, and stimulate discussion. I sent the following letter to students via email and strongly encouraged them to forward it to their parents.

Dear Students & Parents,

In addition to making music, the Cornell Wind Symphony is devoted to the exploration of music as a vehicle for cultural exchange and global awareness. In doing so, students learn the value of applying their discipline's knowledge base to address cultural and societal issues. They realize the potential for a group to become more powerful than the sum of their individual identities. They gain skills in communication, leadership, and collaboration, and employ those skills to engage more broadly and deeply as members of a global community.

In January 2017, the Wind Symphony will embark on a ten-day community-engaged performance tour of Haiti and the Dominican Republic. Over four days in Haiti, we will collaborate with over 100 musicians from The Holy Trinity Music School and perform in concerts staged in the country's two largest cities, Port-au-Prince and Cap-Haitien. After traveling by coach to Santo Domingo, we will spend two days rehearsing and performing with the Carol Morgan High School band.

This tour will result from considerable planning and fruitful partnerships with numerous individuals and organizations, both on campus and in our host countries. Over two visits to both Haiti and the Dominican Republic, I have stayed at all of our chosen hotels and visited all of our performance venues. Preparatory activities will also play an important role in Wind Symphony rehearsals throughout the upcoming semester. Students will learn about the history, culture, and music of both countries; learn essential words and phrases in Haitian Creole and French; and become familiar with community engagement and associated concepts and practices.

Safety is, of course, a primary concern, and every part of the itinerary is being considered with the goal of mitigating risk and ensuring a safe and positive experience. In short, I feel very comfortable with our travel plans, but please do not hesitate to contact me if you have any questions or concerns.

Every member of our ensemble is equally important, and I feel strongly that no one should forego this tour for financial reasons. While most of our expenses will be covered by monetary and in-kind donations, students will be responsible for contributing approximately $800. I understand this may be challenging financially, and soon after the outset of the fall semester, I will guide students through the process of applying for travel aid from the appropriate office on campus. I will invite students to meet with me individually, and all conversations will be held in strict confidence. On a related note, we will soon begin a crowdfunding campaign, and I hope you will consider supporting this endeavor.

As with any recruitment initiative, our students are often our best promoters and ambassadors. After a successful tour experience, use alumni comments to inform current students and their parents. This was especially helpful when traveling to Haiti for the second time in 2019 when the country was assigned a level four travel advisory by the U.S. State Department. The following is one such statement from a student who participated in the 2017 tour.

I never felt unsafe in Haiti or the Dominican Republic. We were escorted by police whenever we traveled through Port-au-Prince, and a security escort stayed with us on the bus at all times. Both of our hotels were well-guarded, and I felt at home in both places. I ate everything provided and never got sick. With regards to health, the Cornell Travel Clinic was very thorough in providing the proper precautions about avoiding (especially food- and water-borne) illness. Being so well-prepared in advance (having bug spray, hand sanitizer, various medications, etc.) was extremely helpful in addressing many of the prevailing concerns about traveling to Haiti and the DR, and I was well-equipped to handle any minor health issues that cropped up amongst myself and others.

Raise Funds and Awareness

Before considering fundraising initiatives, secure permission to do so from your administrators and your institution's development or gift office. Prepare for these conversations by writing a clear and concise budget and targeting individuals or entities that might be interested in supporting the tour. Your school or department may be in a position to offer funds. Additionally, a community-engaged performance tour may appeal to myriad internal and external sources for which a traditional performance tour would not be interesting. To put this in perspective, consider the following two tour proposals and lists of potential supporters.

- **Proposal 1**: A seven-day performance tour of regional high schools featuring performances for relevant student ensembles (e.g., bands and choirs) and culminating in a performance at Carnegie Hall.
  - **Rationale**: The tour is designed to share music; advertise the department or school of music, and the university; recruit students; and

provide current students with a capstone performance in a prestigious venue.
- **Potential supporters**: Department or school of music; alumni of your program; and individual donors interested in supporting musical initiatives
- **Proposal 2**: A seven-day community-engaged performance tour of Haiti and the Dominican Republic.
- **Rationale**: The tour is designed to share music, consider disciplinary content in a global context, generate a reciprocal campus–community partnership, support our institution's goals of global awareness and community engagement, and support goals specified by our community partners.
- **Potential supporters**: Department or school of music; alumni of your program; individual donors interested in supporting musical initiatives; individual donors interested in community engagement initiatives; offices of community engagement, global learning, or service-learning; office of diversity, equity, and inclusion; office of teaching innovation or program development; external grants focused on music and/or the arts; and external grants focused on campus–community engagement.

Most potential donors will likely envisage a tour similar to the first of the aforementioned proposals. You may need to educate and motivate them to support a different approach to touring. Prepare to describe the differences between traditional and community-engaged performance tours, and articulate how the latter type of tour will benefit your students, your institution, and your community partners. Prepare to champion your program.

Fundraising can further your tour goals by generating financial support, stimulating public awareness, and enhancing student enthusiasm. With that in mind, select fundraising projects to achieve one or more objectives. For example, isolated student-led projects such as candy sales or leaf-raking will probably raise a relatively insignificant amount of money, but they may generate valuable word-of-mouth support, potentially leading to individual donations. Additionally, a crowdfunding campaign will be a superior tool for sustained fundraising. If your institution does not have an existing crowdfunding platform, ask permission to advertise your tour on one of the many reputable websites. Consider asking each student to take responsibility for soliciting donations from 15 people. With your students' help, write a statement to be used in phone or email communications, and ask students to adapt it to suit their relationships with potential donors. While you should supervise the project, a student committee should ideally provide the leadership. Fundraising is not a curricular project and should not have grading implications. Your students must be self-motivated and invested in the process to achieve a desirable result.

Prepare Students for Vaccinations and Travel Medications

Health concerns, such as immunizations and medications, require your attention approximately eight weeks before the tour. Fortunately, you will find numerous helpful resources for the public and likely for members of your campus community. Create a password-protected online folder on your institution's web-based course management system (e.g., Canvas or Blackboard) or in a cloud storage platform such as Google Drive. Compile links to relevant websites. In the U.S., begin with the Centers for Disease Control and Prevention (CDC) destination page to gain general information about vaccination requirements. Notify your in-house health center or travel office, and request individual student appointments with a physician or nurse at least six weeks before departure. This will allow ample time for appointment scheduling and vaccines or immunizations that may be required. Students who wish to see their family physician should be encouraged to do so, but the appointment with a professional who is also acting as a school representative should be mandatory.

Establish a secure online travel register to be completed no later than two weeks prior to departure. Your institution may have an existing platform for such a register. Every participant should upload the following documents and information:

- color copy of their passport and visa, if applicable;
- information for at least two emergency contacts;
- copy of personal insurance card;
- list of all food allergies and intolerances (labeled as such).

In the U.S., the Health Insurance Portability and Accountability Act (HIPAA) regulations protect the privacy and security of certain health information, including prescription medications. However, students may need to carry such medications on tour, some of which might be unlicensed or unavailable in the travel location. Urge students to speak with a health professional as appropriate, pack enough medicine for the entire tour, pack copies of all written prescriptions, and leave a copy of prescriptions with at least one of their emergency contacts. Medications should be in carry-on baggage; checked luggage is susceptible to being lost or delayed. You and/or a chaperone should pack a basic travel kit, including common over-the-counter medicines and bandages. Upon completing their registration, you may wish to have students sign a general, non-binding statement verifying that they have made the necessary preparations. The following statement was used for Cornell Wind Symphony tours.

> In submitting my travel documents, I verify that I have:
>
> - assessed my immunization and healthcare needs based on our travel itinerary and my personal health history;
> - verified and obtained all required immunizations (including printed information and documentation);
> - learned about prevention and treatment information for commonly encountered health problems in our tour locations (i.e., food and water precautions, mosquito-borne illness, sun protection, immunizations, and other relevant concerns);
> - acquired personal medications and relevant prescriptions.

Make Arrangements for Students With Disabilities

Students with disabilities should be encouraged to disclose their disability before submitting their travel deposit. Despite your best efforts to accommodate students with disabilities, other countries may not have the capacity to provide accessibility accommodations that they will expect or need. You will need time to work with your community partners and determine what, if any, arrangements are possible. The following questions, adapted from the Cornell Student Disability Services Guide to International Travel (n.d.), are for students to ask themselves if they believe they may require accommodation.

- What accommodations do I think I'll need to live in the country or participate in the program (consider academic, work-related, physical access, housing, transportation, and dietary)?
- How many days and/or weeks do I think I can consecutively travel and live abroad without compromising my physical or mental health and medical or disability needs?
- Am I comfortable disclosing my disability and/or accommodation needs on applications or in the destination country, if asked?

Students should be strongly encouraged to inquire about or research the following questions, depending on their disability. References should include the appropriate on-campus offices, healthcare providers, and information from your community partners.

- What are the host country's perceptions or views of individuals with disabilities?
- What is the host country's definition of "accessible," and does it match what I am used to or need?

- What is the host country's disability law, if any?
- What is the host program's ability to fund the provision of accommodations, if needed?
- What are the housing options, and are they conducive to my needs?
- What are the cultural norms around interpersonal relations and verbal/nonverbal communication, and could they pose any challenges, given my disability?
- How will I maintain my health and disability management schedule, particularly in maintaining a proper medication schedule and continuing physical or mental health appointments/care either in-country or from a distance?
- Is it a country where I can carry medication on my person when traveling there OR ship medication into, and if not, how can I ensure I have the medication or can access the refills I need while there?
- If I anticipate needing mental health services, counseling, or physical rehabilitation services while there, will I be able to access that, and from where/who?
- What is the climate like, and will it be conducive to my condition or exacerbate it?
- What types of food are typically eaten in-country, and are they conducive to my dietary needs?

Final Thoughts

The aforementioned steps will help you plan and lead a safe, secure tour for your ensemble. Nevertheless, it is impossible to anticipate every issue or plan for every contingency. Even when we do our best to design the best possible experience, circumstances beyond our control may force us to make decisions that may detract from our mission or undermine our goals. The following is one such case.

As described earlier, the second Cornell Wind Symphony (CWS) tour of Haiti and the Dominican Republic in January 2019 was subject to numerous unforeseen complications resulting from political instability in both Haiti and the U.S. A few months before the tour, the U.S. State Department raised a Level Two travel advisory for Haiti to Level Three ("reconsider travel"). After consulting with my community partners, I traveled to Haiti individually, and together we judged that we could meet our goals and ensure a safe experience for our students. Upon returning home, I presented the situation to my students and university travel advisors, and we decided to continue with the tour, albeit with extra safety and security precautions in place. As one example, Richard Morse, proprietor of the Oloffson Hotel, agreed to accommodate us should we need to shelter in place.

The U.S. federal government shut down when the pieces seemed to come together. Totaling 35 days, it was the most protracted U.S. government shutdown in history. Approximately one-fourth of government activities were affected. Nonessential U.S. personnel exited Haiti, and those that remained were authorized to perform limited official engagements. The government closure led to the cancellation of a scheduled performance at the residence of the U.S. Ambassador to the Republic of Haiti and prompted the withdrawal of associated financial support and publicity. This financial loss exacerbated a shortfall resulting from lackluster fundraising campaigns by both the CWS and the Holy Trinity Music School (HTMS). As a result, the two organizations could not share travel and lodging expenses as we did in the previous tour. Moreover, I was required to hire only vendors willing and able to provide the necessary insurance documents and levels of accommodations. The result was an uneven distribution of privileges between the CWS and HTMS and far fewer opportunities for our students to gather informally and socialize.

When the two organizations traveled from Port-au-Prince to the southern coastal city of Jacmel, the CWS traveled in coaches, and HTMS traveled in school buses. HTMS joined us a day later because they could not afford an additional night of accommodations (Cornell could not help). While the two student populations ultimately enjoyed a similar standard of accommodations, they stayed at different hotels and rarely interacted outside of rehearsals. This situation had an immediate, negative, and lasting impact on our combined social, cultural, and musical outcomes. Members of the CWS who had participated in the previous tour were candid in their assessment that they felt awkwardly disconnected from their Haitian colleagues and the location itself. One student recalled:

> The last time we were in Haiti, everything was so novel to me: the sights, the sounds, the food, the people. And we got to spend lots of time rehearsing and bonding with the students from HTMS, which was very rewarding. Combined with our crazy misadventures, the 2017 trip was truly an unforgettable experience. And so, as we traveled back to Haiti for the second time in two years, I expected us to have more wild adventures while we continued to maintain and improve our ongoing relationship with the people at HTMS. But I couldn't help but feel that the trip was lacking; early on, all leisure time with the students, and all but one rehearsal, were canceled for various logistical and financial reasons (in part due to the U.S. government shutdown). As a result, we had enough free time for the trip to feel, at times, like a vacation. I felt frustrated that we were traveling around in our bland bubble. We strolled around picturesque seaside locations outside of cushy hotels and discussed our feelings about Haitian history and politics. It felt as though we were treating the whole country as a museum. I felt as though some of the interpersonal and human elements that made the last trip so great were lost.
>
> (Michael Zhou, 2019)

After reading my student's reflection, I resolved to try to find a "sweet spot" between the 2017 and 2019 tours during the final CWS tour of Haiti in 2021. As listed earlier, numerous circumstances forced us to cancel that tour, and, in light of the current political climate in Haiti, it will be impossible to travel there for the foreseeable future.

Notes

1 Information can be found in the American Psychological Association's *Inclusive language guidelines* (2020). www.apa.org/about/apa/equity-diversity-inclusion/language-guidelines.pdf
2 Students enrolled in the Cornell Wind Symphony earn one academic credit. An additional optional credit is made available for the semester prior to the tour, which takes place during winter break. This credit compensates students for additional learning activities, individual work, and the tour itself. As of this writing, the U.S. Department of Education defines a credit hour as an amount of work "that reasonably approximates not less than one hour of classroom or direct faculty instruction and a minimum of two hours of out of class work each week for approximately fifteen weeks for one semester . . . or the equivalent amount of work over a different period of time" (Electronic Code of Federal Regulations, 2022).

References

Cornell University Student Disability Services. (n.d.). *Guide to international travel.* https://sds.cornell.edu/resources/guide-international-travel
Electronic Code of Federal Regulations. (2022). *Institutional eligibility under the higher education act of 1965, as amended.* www.ecfr.gov/current/title-34/subtitle-B/chapter-VI/part-600/subpart-A/section-600.2

Epilogue

The COVID-19 (coronavirus) pandemic brought performance tours to a virtual standstill. D'Eramo writes that "the pandemic proved the centrality of tourism through tourism's omission" (2017, p. 9). This was also true for tours within the context of Cornell Wind Symphony (CWS) community engagement initiatives. The CWS last toured Haiti and the Dominican Republic in January 2019. As of this writing, only one member of the current ensemble participated in one of those tours. All of the groundwork to educate the students and help them develop cultural competency, the developed and refined practical and logistical practices and materials, and the enthusiasm surrounding our campus–community partnership has fallen away. The slate has been wiped clean. My partners and I tried to keep our collaboration alive through virtual engagements; however, while beneficial, they were not a viable alternative to in-person connections in tour locations. Community-engaged performance tours enable university students to escape their day-to-day campus existence, develop cultural competency through lived experience in the community, and engage with community partners by making music with them—live and in-person. Adjunctive projects can help sustain the partnership between tours but cannot substitute for tours.

As stated earlier, the CWS will not be able to return to Haiti in the foreseeable future due to severe political instability and civil unrest. On behalf of Cornell, I will join The Rev. Stephen Davenport[1] in establishing a CWS-HTMS online connection program, which will include establishing high-speed Internet at the HTMS campus in Port-au-Prince, the donation and setup of relevant hardware, and the use of readily available videoconferencing software. We hope to use the platform to facilitate peer-to-peer student connections, and teacher training sessions involving HTMS faculty and Cornell applied wind instrument and percussion instructors.

Simultaneously, I have begun to establish new partnerships with musical organizations based in San Germán, San Juan, and Yauco, Puerto Rico, with the goal of touring those locations in January 2023. While I look forward to these new possibilities, it saddens me to suspend ensemble tours to Haiti. My

DOI: 10.4324/9781003278696-8

experiences there are among my fondest musical memories, and I will always cherish my relationships with my community partners.

Richard Morse, founder and director of RAM, was introduced earlier in this book. I recently asked Richard to speak about RAM's two residencies at Cornell's Ithaca campus, and to describe the ways in which the Cornell partnership helped him further the band's goals.

You came to the Oloffson Hotel in Haiti with the Cornell Wind Symphony in 2017. When you heard RAM, you picked up on a vibe that made you want to dig farther. That was important to me. The fact that you were intrigued enough to bring us to Cornell meant a lot to me and to the musicians of RAM. You direct a classical ensemble. You make classical music in the Western European tradition. We make music of the people. Back in the day, snobs disrespected the music and the culture we promote. Your musicians read sheet music and learn the music in weekly rehearsals. Our musicians learn music in eight-hour gigs on the street. It's rote and repetition. It's different than classroom learning. The fact that a classical ensemble came together and wanted to learn about Haitian folklore and culture and music was big to me. To me, this is Haiti's classical music. The songs are Haiti's classical songs. The rhythms are complex and sophisticated. The music that came out of the Western hemisphere—jazz, blues, and related genres—draws on the rhythms and the melodic structures of Haitian music.

The residencies at Cornell helped us by bringing our music into an academic setting. We do that whenever possible; when we're in a town, I reach out to local schools and talk to anyone interested in learning about the music. That's what we do. And you also helped us by filling out dates on our tour calendar [laughs]. And here we are, we're still talking. In spite of the pandemic, with everyone bunkering down, we're still talking.[2]

In a separate conversation, I spoke with The Rev. Stephen Davenport about the ongoing partnership between Cornell and the Holy Trinity Music School (HTMS). Introduced earlier in this book, Stephen has been working with Haitian individuals and institutions since 1970. In addition to his work in Haiti, beginning in 1996, Stephen and The Rev. David César organized more than 250 HTMS concerts in the U.S. and Canada.

I have participated in many HTMS tours of the U.S., but this was my first experience with a U.S. ensemble traveling and performing in Haiti. Back in 2017, it started with joint rehearsals at the HTMS campus in Port-au-Prince. People from both groups intermingled, although neither spoke the other's language. No matter; they both loved the music, and that carried the day. From that point forward, we built on that solid musical foundation.

We traveled six hours or more to get to Cap-Haïtian. We performed together in the beautiful ruins of Palais Sans-Souci, under the evening sky of the seaside city of Jacmel, in the Kiosk Occide Jeanty in Port-au-Prince, and in St. Etienne Episcopal Church in the mountains of Buteau. In all cases, the mission was the same: young people offering music and sharing the joy of making music. Music is a realm wherein a person can create beauty. And, in an ensemble, one makes music with others. And we enabled them to perform together, and to share their creation with others.

It means so much for the Haitians that people to care enough to come to visit their island. They cannot leave their country without a visa, and visas from Haiti are almost impossible to get. Most Haitians are born in Haiti, live in Haiti, and die in Haiti without ever leaving the country, without being able to experience the world. It is tremendously important to see that the world is bigger than oneself. This is what Cornell brought to the partnership. You performed for all sorts of people, from the Prime Minister in Port-au-Prince to people who have never left—and will likely never leave—their village in the mountains. You helped them see the wider world. In the overall partnership, Cornell and HTMS had the privilege of being guests in each other's country. That created a meaningful and bond—one that has benefited everyone involved.[3]

Community-engaged performance tours offer benefits unobtainable using traditional tour models. These benefits—for me, my students, the ensemble, and our community partners—have inspired me to make community engagement an integral part of my teaching philosophy. The tours have enabled me to celebrate the students as people by fostering their social, cultural, and musical competencies. My students have learned about themselves by considering their positionality and the context that creates their identity. They have addressed and begun to unpack broad and complex global issues, including climate change, discrimination, Eurocentrism, colonialism, and axes of power and privilege. These personal changes have led to a clear and compelling change in the ensemble's learning culture: students who participated in the tour have become more collegial and caring. They have taken a greater interest in each other as individuals and embraced the many benefits of any collaborative endeavor. One of my students wrote:

> I can see where things like musical and cultural exchange stand in the unbelievably fuzzy mess of Haitian and American current events, and I can appreciate the opportunity that we had, and the lives that we interacted with (if only briefly). At the end of the day, human connection—however fleeting it may be—really is the most important aspect of our lives. Maybe a cliché thing to say, but I believe it to my core.
>
> (Meghna Srivastava, 2019)

Epilogue 107

As an ensemble director, I often work with students throughout their entire undergraduate experience. I have the privilege of observing their growth and maturation. Community-engaged performance tours make a clear and lasting impact on students' lives. I hope this book will inspire readers to plan and lead such a tour.

Notes

1 The Rev. Davenport was introduced earlier in this book. He is a longtime supporter of Haitian institutions and is presently responsible for the U.S. nonprofit, The Friends of the Holy Trinity Music School.
2 Richard Morse, interview by author, October 10, 2022.
3 The Rev. Stephen Davenport III, interview by author, September 17, 2022.

Reference

D'Eramo, M. (2017). *The world in a selfie: An inquiry into the tourist age.* Verso.

Appendix A
Selected Journaling Guidelines, Prompts, and Questions

Journaling is a kind of writing that encompasses concrete observations, feelings, and thoughts to document and reflect on lived experiences. In contrast, a field notebook has a more externally-focused documentary purpose and often includes drawings and found objects (e.g., grasses and leaves). A travel journal is a mix of these two genres; it includes a documentary of encounters with another culture (noting both experiences and observations), recollections of interactions with peers and community partners, and miscellany including drawings, feelings, personally important moments, and confessions.

Anchored in the belief that writing is thinking and that our thinking changes, grows, and deepens through reflection, a travel journal kept before, during, and after the tour can augment learning. Before travel, documenting and reflecting on expectations and fears, having an opportunity to make predictions, thinking in advance about how to manage stress and strong emotions, and setting personal learning goals can help one feel more prepared to arrive more open-minded, curious, and ready for the encounter with another culture. During the tour, journaling helps students revisit, critique, and consider their feelings and observations. After the tour, students can describe what they learned, explore lingering questions, and further develop their capacities for intercultural understanding (Hartman et al., 2018).

Organizing and stimulating the journaling process through prompts can help students focus on the process, spur creativity, and deepen reflection and learning. When the writing is shared, it can indicate where coaching or guided interventions might be helpful. The writing may support group learning, and it can be used to generate ideas for blogs or formal responses.

Ensemble directors should commit to journaling along with the students. Even if the writing is not shared, it will foster an empathetic understanding of the students' assignments. Remind students that, while rehearsals and performances are collaborative endeavors, journaling is for their individual benefit. Encourage them to turn off their inner critic and permit themselves to write freely and uncritically. The journal entries will not be evaluated; they exist only to foster personal growth by documenting observations, stimulating emotional reactions, and potentially fostering unexpected connections. With effort and a measure of diligence, journaling can become a regular habit and valuable resource for developing and reflecting upon perspectives and ideas. The following journaling prompts are adapted from the Cornell University Off-Campus International Activity Toolkit.[1]

Pre-tour

- Begin by responding to the following questions. Don't overthink your answers; simply listen to yourself, and honestly record your thoughts and emotions about the tour. How do you feel? What are your expectations? What are your fears?
- Write about your coping skills. How do you handle change and stress? Tell an anecdote or two. What makes you feel better?
- Select a quote from a poem, novel, or famous person from the country you are traveling to or are already visiting and write a response that engages the quote. Share your quote with others and swap quotes. Alternative: Find a local proverb or a few lines from a local song, and respond to it.
- Why are stereotypes dangerous? Write about one that relates to the place you're visiting and talk about what it means and in what ways it might be harmful.
- Reflect on a few of your core values. Do you anticipate any of your values being challenged while on tour? Think about how you have bridged differences in the past.
- Respond to a newspaper headline that reminds you of something you care about or that seems strange, unjust, untrue, or dangerous. Find out more information about the story.
- Write a response to a statement that shows understanding for more than one point of view. For example, "tourism is unethical."

On Tour

- Jot down a list of concrete, sensory details: what do you/did you see, smell, hear, touch, taste? These types of lists can jog your memory later, can help you distill the experience, and can provide a break from the work of creating a narrative. The list can also lead to other projects: poems, collages, and other creative projects.
- For a given day, write about a high, a low, and a question.
- Write down an observation. Formulate a more generalized hypothesis based on your observation. Generate a question about your hypothesis. Then share your three items with a local or a person who is a cultural expert and "test" your hypothesis. Let your interlocutor respond to your hypothesis. Just listen. Ask clarifying questions if necessary. Then, go back and write down the insider's response—try to be true to their words.

Then write a reaction to their ideas. Revise your hypothesis based on the new information you received.
- Journal outside on location to write a concrete description of your environment. Engage multiple senses to capture a fuller, multidimensional picture. Capture bits of speech. Sketch landscapes or people. Tell your inner critic to be quiet.
- Respond to a photograph, artwork, or music from the area and respond to it in writing: first describe, then evaluate, then interpret—try to withhold interpretation before really looking. Seek more information to answer any questions that may have come up for you during the exercise.
- Observe a conversation between two people. Write about what you observed. How did each person help keep the conversation going? What clues did you gather about status, class, position and power, personalities, pacing, appropriate ways to interrupt, excuse, etc., and other cultural information that might help understand this culture?
- Over several days, look out for examples of empathy, curiosity, misunderstandings, patterns of behavior you don't understand, gender expectations, mysteries, or any other list of arbitrary characteristics or culturally relevant markers, and write a reflection on these as you anchor your reflection within your cultural context. Investigate some of your findings and reflect further.
- Write about "rich" moments—any moments of embarrassment, misunderstanding, miscommunication, awkwardness, or a misreading of others.
- Ask your hosts about their cultural and national identities. Write about what you learn.

Post-tour Reflection

- How has this journey made you feel about your own cultural and national identities?
- Draft a letter to someone who may never have the experience of going to this place. Letters inspire a different tone, more organized thinking, and sometimes better descriptions when describing what we are seeing to someone who may never have the experience.
- Respond to a brochure or tourist literature about the place you are visiting. Challenge or clarify stereotypes, oversimplifications, or attempts to make the place seem exotic. Try to find more than one perspective.
- Write about: 1) something you learned that you didn't know before, 2) something that surprised you, and 3) a question raised for you that didn't get answered.
- Develop a pithy response for friends and family who may label the community partners' location or culture with stereotypes.

Note

1 Cornell University Center for Teaching Innovation. (n.d.). *Active learning in online teaching*. https://teaching.cornell.edu/resource/active-learning-online-teaching

Appendix B
Sample Reflection Exercise: The Identity Pie

A community-engaged performance tour can be used as a vehicle for students to become more aware of their position and worldview, to identify aspects of the culture with which they identify, and to explore how their worldview informs their beliefs, values, behaviors, and sense of self. It can highlight how culture defines who we are, how we understand ourselves and others, and the misperceptions we might have about our own or others' cultural identity and assumptions. It can provide a forum for processing complex social constructs, such as race and religion. Of course, this will not happen organically. As stated earlier in this book, reflection exercises should be an integral part of group activities before, during, and after the tour.

As described by Hartman et al. (2018), the *identity pie* is an exercise that focuses on the social construction of identity, as well as the socially structured dimensions of power relations. It is designed to help students develop an understanding of the aforementioned concepts, and explore the norms and beliefs of the culture they will engage with while on tour. The activity should be completed as a group, but it can also be repeated with community partners on location. The following are sample instructions for students:

- Write down five to ten visible and/or invisible aspects of your individual culture and identity.
- Using the shape of a pie, draw how the attributes you've listed constitute your identity. Larger slices of the pie represent more dominant aspects of your identity.
- Be prepared to share your drawing with a partner and/or the group.
- Note: You need not necessarily use the pie as a metaphor for drawing, but you should draw the things that you feel compose your cultural identity.

After students have generated their responses, initiate a discussion about the items they documented. If students are reluctant to share their work, consider beginning with a variation of the "pair and share" activity described earlier in this book. Remind students that the tour group is safe and free from judgment, and that they should feel free to withhold items that they are not comfortable sharing. For each item, ask students to clarify its meaning and the role it plays in their life. This will help students thoughtfully consider the attribute and articulate its importance to them. Students should be encouraged to speak only to their own experience and avoid generalizations. Follow-up discussion could focus on power and privilege relations among individuals and groups; or the relationship between dominant cultural values, assumptions, and norms and an individual's culture and identity.

Regardless of the topic of discussion, this and many other reflection exercises have the potential to elicit beliefs, feelings, and perceptions that may be sensitive and highly personal. The facilitator must proceed carefully, consistently monitor the temperature of the room, and be ready to respond in kind. It is also important to conclude the activity by relating the discussion to the tour and the students' engagement with community partners. As one example, students could explore ways in which they might respond if confronted with different cultural beliefs or norms, or unpack a complicated or confusing cross-cultural experience.

Reference

Hartman, E., Kiely, R., Friedrichs, J., & Boettcher, C. (2018). *Community-based global learning: The theory and practice of ethical engagement at home and abroad.* Stylus Publishing.

Index

accommodations 82–83
AFCEA Tour Consultants 30
Agricultural College Act *see* Morrill Land Grant Acts
AmeriCorps 12
anxiety 39
Astin, A. W. 51

Bank, Russell 79
Baron Cimetiére 79
Benchmarks for Campus Community Partnerships 35, 37
Biggs, J. B. 58, 64
Bloom, Benjamin 56
Bonaparte, Napoleon 69
Boyer, Ernest 15
Buber, Martin 28–29
budgets 93–94, 97–98

Campus Compact 13, 16, 18n4, 35
Carol Morgan School 72, 73, 77, 87
César, David 4–5, 68, 74, 85–87
challenging context 40
Christoph, Henri 89n12
citizens 37–38
Classical Movements 30
colleges and universities 8–12 *see also* education
colonialism 18n3
communication 60–61, 96–97
community engagement: benefits of 106; democratic 51; developing partnerships 40–44, 71–74; methods of 31–32; and scholarship 15–17 *see also* performance tours
conductors 51–52, 59–60
constructivism 46–49
content 49, 52–54

Continental Drift (Bank) 79
Cornell University 67
Cornell Wind Symphony: about 67; communication with families 96–97; forming community partnerships 71–74; future plans of 104; in Haiti 1–3; planning tours 67–69; purpose of 37; syllabus 51, 55, 93–95; tour itinerary 74–76
COVID-19 4, 87, 104
Crichton, S. 40
Crucible Moment, A 16
Cuba 80
cultural competencies 23, 25–26, 28, 30, 80, 84–86 *see also* society and culture

Danzón No. 2 (Márquez) 80
Davenport, Stephen 68, 74, 85–86, 104, 105–106
Deardorff, D. K. 23
DeGraff, M. 70
democracy 51–52, 65
D'Eramo, Marco 104
Dewey, John 24–25, 47
Dierking, L. D. 24
Dominican Republic 68, 72
Dubois, Laurent 78
Duvalier, François "Papa Doc" 89n8

education 9–10, 13–15, 17, 24–27 *see also* colleges and universities
Educational World Tours 30
1804 (Jeanty) 77
Eisenhower, Dwight D. 12
emotions 62–63
Enos, S. 35
ethnicity 26–27

ethnomusicology 53–54
evaluations 50, 58–59
experiential learning 24–25, 46–49
Eyler, J. 49

France 69
Friere, Paulo 47, 50, 65n1
Fulbright, J. William 12

gentility 8–9
GI Bill 12
Gmelch, G. 25–26
Grantham, Donald 80
Guillaume, Sydney 77–78

Haiti: current conditions in 4, 68–70, 84–85, 87–88; elevated risk in 81–82, 101; engagement with 56–59, 71–74; experience of 102; history and culture 3–4, 69–70, 77–79, 88; logistics in 1–3; music in 77–78; perception of 78
Haitian Fight Song (Mingus) 77
Holy Trinity Music School 71, 72–73, 86–87, 88, 101

Ich und Du (Buber) 28–29
Indigenous populations 11, 18n2
Inhelder, B. 26

Jacoby, B. 14, 48
Jeanty, Occide 77, 88n5
Jefferson, Thomas 69
Johnson, Lyndon 12–13

Kahne, J. 37
Katz, Jonathan 84
Kellogg Commission 16
Kennedy, John F. 12–13
Kolb, David 25, 48, 62

land acknowledgments 11
learner-centered teaching 49–59
Learner-Centered Teaching (Weimer) 49
learning 50, 55–58
Lincoln, Abraham 9

MacCannell, D. 29
Magic Island, The (Seabrook) 78
Mambo (Grantham) 80
Márquez, Arturo 80
Mingus, Charles 77

mission statements 36–39
mizik rasin 72
Moise, Jovenal 4
Morrill Land Grant Acts 9–11, 16, 18n1
Morrill, Justin 9
Morse, Richard 72, 78, 86, 101, 105
Morton, K. 35
Mouton, W. 25
Mozart, Wolfgang Amadeus 27
music: and culture 52–54, 78–80, 89n10; selecting 77–78

National Society of Experiential Education (NSEE) 13–14
National Task Force on Civic Learning and Democratic Engagement 16

Oloffson Hotel 71–72, 83
Onguko, B. 40

partnerships: development of 40–44, 104–105; importance of 35–36; types of 35–36
Peace Corps 12
pedagogy 46, 50–52
performance tours: administration approval of 90–91; benefits of 5–6, 21–23, 106; budgeting for 93–94; as commodities 29–30; and community partnerships 35–36; in course syllabus 93–95; and educating students 76–77; in elevated risk locations 81–82; fundraising 97–98; itinerary 74–76, 91; location selection 27–28, 39–40, 67–70; planning 8, 40–44; purpose of 37; and tourism 27–29; and travel companies 44–45 *see also* community engagement
philosophy 36–40
Piaget, J. 26, 47
Pink, Daniel 39
Plessy v. Ferguson 10
power 49–52
Pythagoras 53–54

RAM 72, 73, 86–87, 105
Ramsey, William 13
reflection 59–65
religion 18n1
Renesans (Guillaume) 77–78

repertoire 52–54
Robinson, M. 26, 27

Seabrook, William 78
service-learning 13–16, 18n5
Sigmon, Robert 13
Smith, M. 26, 27
social classes 8–9, 10–11
social justice 12–13
society and culture: definition 23; engagement with 25–26, 53; and higher education 17; and music 78–80; stereotypes 25–26; and tourism 27–28 *see also* cultural competencies
Sorber, N. M. 10
student-centered learning *see* learner-centered teaching

Taxonomy for Teaching, Learning, and Assessment, A (Bloom) 56
teachers 50, 54–55
Tompkins, J. 50–51
tourism: and community engagement 31–32; cultural 27–28; and cultural misconceptions 25–26; definition 27; and education 24–27; and performance tours 27–29; results of 29
transportation 83–84
travel: accommodations for students with disabilities 100–101; arrangements 92; benefits of 22–23; and education 25, 76–77; preparation for 99–100; and tourism 24
travel companies 44–45

universities *see* colleges and universities

Vodou 78–79, 89n7, 89n9
volunteerism: and community partnerships 37; principles of 13–14; vs. service 38, 67–68

Weimer, Maryellen 49
Westheimer, J. 37
What Kind of Citizen? (Westheimer and Kahne) 37
White Zombie 78
Wood, R. E. 26
World War II 12

For Product Safety Concerns and Information please contact our EU
representative GPSR@taylorandfrancis.com
Taylor & Francis Verlag GmbH, Kaufingerstraße 24, 80331 München, Germany